The COMMON LAW

Geoffrey Gibson has practised law as a member of the firm that is now Ashurst and the Victorian Bar. He has trained and practised in mediation and arbitration in Australia and the USA. Since conducting a public inquiry in 1992, he has practised substantially in tribunal work. He presided over a state tax tribunal for 18 years and currently holds statutory appointments. He has had more than fifty decisions published in law reports. His decisions have reached the High Court on five occasions. He has published extensively on the failings of our law. This is his fifth book on the law.

The COMMON LAW
A History

Geoffrey Gibson

AUSTRALIAN SCHOLARLY

© Geoffrey Gibson 2012

First published 2012, by Australian Scholarly Publishing Pty Ltd
7 Lt Lothian St Nth, North Melbourne, Vic 3051   TEL: 03 9329 6963   FAX: 03 9329 5452
EMAIL: aspic@ozemail.com.au   WEB: scholarly.info

ISBN 978-1-921875-66-3

ALL RIGHTS RESERVED

Cover illustration: Sir William Blackstone

Design and typesetting Art Rowlands   *Printing and binding* BPA Print Group
This book is typeset in Adobe Garamond Pro 11/21pt

In memory of Jim Kennan

Contents

Foreword		*ix*
I.	Prelude: Ancient Law	1
II.	The German Influence	11
III.	The Norman Connection	17
IV.	Magna Carta	25
V.	The Birth of Equity	32
VI.	A Profession for Lawyers	41
VII.	Crime, Contract, and Negligence	56
VIII.	The Constitutional Settlement	68
IX.	Judges and Jurists	77
X.	Law and Morals	96
XI.	Postlude: Real Decline and Likely Fall	110
Chronology		*129*
Notes		*130*
References		*134*
List of Cases		*136*
Index		*137*

Foreword

About a century and a half ago, Sir Henry Maine wrote a book on legal history called *Ancient Law: its connection with the early history of society, and its relation to modern ideas*. Its chief object was the same as the chief object of this book – to look at the history of a body of law and to point out how that body of law relates to ours.

I have two motives. First, about forty years practice at the law as counsel, attorney, and hearing cases, and occasionally writing about and teaching the law, leaves me with the clear view that you cannot understand our law unless you understand its history.

Secondly, and relatedly, we are currently destroying our heritage and jeopardizing the future of those who come after us. Through our ignorance of our history, we are not doing enough to protect our future.

I will confine myself to the texts that I regard as paramount for the history of English law so that anyone interested can pursue further inquiry fairly simply. All the texts, including Holdsworth's *History of English Law*, *State Trials* and the *Year Books*, are in my own library, either at Malmsbury or Owen Dixon Chambers. Where I have felt it necessary to refer to a citation, I have done so in the Notes (using abbreviations in bold in the References) or in the List of Cases at the end of the book. Other Codes and texts referred to are easily accessible on the Web.

Unlike Maine, I will try to avoid old words and dead languages – Maine wrote when gentlemen were expected to know both Greek and

Latin – but like Maine I will avoid dates and footnotes. I share his 'disrelish', one of his favourite words, for both. Dates may be found in the chronology at the end of the text and, as indicated, any necessary citations will be given in the Notes.

The laws of our own ancestors were mainly concerned with land and cattle ownership, and the status of people. This history focuses on procedure, as is the wont of the common law. On substance, it will not be directed at property or status, which are mainly now regulated by statute, but the five areas essential to understanding our common law: constitutional law, crime, equity, contract, and negligence.

The scholarship on English legal history is unbelievably rich, both in England and the United States of America. We are blessed with names like Ames, Cardozo, Dicey, Holdsworth, Holmes, Maine, Maitland, Thayer, Pollock, and Wigmore. In my country, Sir Victor Windeyer, a Justice of the High Court of Australia, was very learned in legal history, and wrote on the subject extensively at a time when all the justices of that court had a deep knowledge of and instinct for the history of the common law.

Well, this attachment to the past is out of fashion now. I would be the first to scrap all the flim-flam of pantomime – the costumes, the ermine and silk, the wigs and bibs, and the rest of the comfy rugs and baby rattles we cling to so desperately – the bowing and scraping and fawning, the titles and the labels and the ceremonials – but if you want to wean lawyers from their history, you will cut off their life blood.

Since we start at Adam and Eve and finish with Armageddon, we will have to compress a little, but what follows is in my view the irreducible minimum required to separate lawyers from money changers.

We lawyers are interested in our history, not just as a source of instruction or comfort, but as a source of obligation. I have referred elsewhere to an observation of Dietrich Bonhoeffer, but I hope I may be excused for doing it again. The mother of his father, Julie Bonhoeffer, had been an outspoken opponent of the Nazis. When the decrees against the Jews were pronounced, when she was aged about 90, she just walked through the Stormtroopers standing outside Jewish

Foreword

shops, saying that she would shop where she had always shopped. She died in 1936. Bonhoeffer preached a sermon at her funeral. In the course of it he said:

> She came out of a different time, out of a different spiritual world, and this world will not shrink into the grave with her. This heritage, for which we are grateful to her, puts us under obligations.

The whole Bonhoeffer family stood for the *noblesse oblige*, a dying institution.

We need not stay to recall what happened when the German people – the people with whom this history properly begins – did not discharge their obligation to their past.

Malmsbury
Melbourne Cup Day 2012
797th Anniversary Year of *Magna Carta*

The law did not begin with a theory. It has never worked one out ... Ignorance is the best of law reformers. People are glad to discuss a question on general principles, when they have forgotten the special knowledge necessary for technical reasoning.

—*Oliver Wendell Holmes*

I have not for many years past believed in what calls itself historical jurisprudence. The only direct utility of legal history (I say nothing of its thrilling interest) lies in the lesson that each generation has an enormous power of shaping its own law. I don't think that the study of legal history should make men fatalists; I doubt it would make them conservatives. I am sure it would free them from superstitions and teach them that they have free hands.

—*F.W. Maitland*

I
Prelude: Ancient Law

> If a man bring an accusation against a man, and charge him with a crime, but cannot prove it, he, the accuser, shall be put to death.
> *The Code of Hammurabi, Article 1*

> What is truth?
> *Pontius Pilate*

Adam and Eve, it is said, were subject to only one law or command from God. They were not to eat of the tree of knowledge. They did so. They were confronted with their offence, convicted and sentenced to the loss of life. Subsequently, it is said, the sentence was commuted. Could you find a simpler case of the law in action and at the very birth of mankind?

Notice two things. First, we see and talk about this ancient fable from our own perspective, and we as lawyers have trouble not discussing it in our own terms, such as 'offence', and 'sentence'. Historians are guilty of doing this all the time, especially legal historians. Milton was a great example. Not only, in his account, did the prosecution move through the steps that we would expect a prosecution to take now, but Milton went further and sent Raphael to give a warning to Adam and Eve. If the warning had been given before the alleged offence, an

English policeman may have called this a 'caution'. An American may have referred to *Miranda*. Milton records that by instructing Raphael to give the warning, the eternal Father 'fulfilled all justice'. However that may be, we have taken complete leave of the source.

Secondly, most people now think of the story of Adam and Eve as a pure myth, as mythological as the description of creation that accompanies its first telling. But it matters not for most readers if this story is said to be grounded in fact. What matters is that the story was told and has lived. It is the same with many of our ancient laws. It matters not if they were badly made, or even if they were made at all. What matters is that they have been acted on and have become part of our legal fabric. Sensible people are bored with the suggestion that a man called Shakespeare may not have written the plays attributed to Shakespeare – what matters is the plays, and the rest is idle chatter. We need not worry now about the legality of *Magna Carta* or the *Bill of Rights*. What matters is how they have shaped our legal thinking and our constitutional history.

In the first page of his book on *Ancient Law*, Sir Henry Maine remarked that the chief reason for the differences between Roman law and English law was that Roman jurisprudence had 'a theoretical descent' from a code, whereas English law had a 'theoretical ascription' to immemorial unwritten tradition. He then proceeded to identify the principal stages of development common to the various bodies of ancient law as follows.

In the first phase, the law consists of little more than judgments given by a king with divine inspiration. What the king gave, at least in the first instance, was a judgment (or 'doom'), not a law; he was a judge, not a law-maker. The source here is Homer, and, Maine says, the word 'law' is not found in Homer. Homer, in the Bronze Age, looked down with characteristically Greek contempt on foreigners (*barbarians*) less civilized than the Greeks, such as those 'lawless brutes', the Cyclops.

> They have no meeting place for council, no laws either.
> No, up on the mountain peaks they live in arching caverns —

each a law to himself, ruling his wives and children.
Not a care in the world for any neighbour.

This looks like a reasonable picture of the dawn of our history. It is a regime just out of chaos, a regime of whim rather than law.

Next, the king gives way to an aristocracy. Its members become the keepers of the law. They are not able to claim divine judgment for each command or decree. Their monopoly is not of divine instruction or inspiration, but of knowledge of the laws.

In the third phase – and these phases clearly overlap – habit becomes custom and custom becomes law, a kind of unwritten law. Take some of the customs that the Greek historian Herodotus observed in Egypt. An Egyptian should not kiss a Greek. If a man accidentally touches a pig, he must plunge into a river fully dressed. There must be no sex in sacred places. Young people should give up their seats for older people. Which of these might harden into a law might depend on whether there was an issue of cleanliness (as in the first two), or religion (the third), but the process would likely be the same. The Pharaoh, or his officer, would make a decree in a given case. Repeated enough, this decree would become a decree in the wider sense. This, we shall see, is the method of the common law.

The next phase is the codes. The best known are those of Hammurabi, *The Laws of Moses*, including the Ten Commandments, *The Laws of Solon* of Athens, *The Twelve Tablets* of Rome, and later the *Corpus Iuris* of Justinian, including the *Code of Justinian*.

This is not the place to analyse the substance of the various Codes, but if you look at the quotation from one of them at the head of this chapter, you know immediately you are not looking at a law made today. For the most part, these Codes were more direct and more simple, and therefore better written, than almost all of the statutes now churned out on a daily basis throughout the entire common law world.

Let us take a few articles of the Code of Hammurabi published in Babylon about 4,000 years ago, a code more sensible and more humane than Iraq would have known for a very long time.

> 7   If a man purchases … anything … from a man's son or a man's servant, or if he receive the same in trust, that man shall be put to death.

> 142   If a woman hate her husband and say 'You shall not have me', they shall inquire into her antecedents and defects; and if she has been a careful mistress and been without reproach, and her husband has been out belittling her, that woman has no blame. She shall receive her dowry and go back to her father's house.

> 143   If she has not been a careful mistress, gadded about and neglected her house, and belittled her husband, they shall throw that woman into the water.

> 244   If a man hire an ox or an ass and a lion kill it in the field, it is the owner's affair.

Notice the way the first of those articles touches on our notions of fiduciary relationship, undue influence, and trust, and the way the two articles relating to women are millennia ahead of their time – or what women could expect anywhere in the Middle East now.

Finally, and on the fiduciary obligation, here is a clause from the twelve tablets published in Rome.

> If a patron defrauds his client, let him be outlawed.

To use a modern term, a code is more transparent – or at least more apparent – than unwritten usage or precedent. It is some form of protection against fraud and abuse by the aristocracy. But the codes get widened in their application by the process of analogy that is deployed by the common law. As a result, prohibition of a specific act for the purposes of promoting cleanliness can descend into ceremonial abstinence or ritual ablution, and a division of people by status can degenerate into 'the most disastrous and blighting of all human institutions, Caste'. These problems are worse where the ruling body, the aristocracy, draws its power from religion rather than politics, or the military. These generalisations are dangerous, but this may be one of the great differences between East and West, that the ruling parties were able to divorce themselves from religion earlier in the West than in the East.

The next phase observed by Maine was what we call 'fictions'. They are a form of pretence. Since family groupings were essential to defining status, it was common for people to resort to fictions to extend the ambit of the claim for family. Families were able to be extended artificially by use of adoption. Fictions came to be prominent in medieval England to enable courts to extend jurisdiction by pretending that a state of affairs existed which would give a court jurisdiction. But the fiction that Maine chose as the primary one for his purposes was the fact that when a decision is given, the law has been to that extent changed, whereas it was, until at least recently, the fiction that the law remained as it always had been. The judges liked the fiction that they did not make the law. They did not want to be seen as law-makers, that is, legislators.

The final phase of the development of these legal bodies lay in legislation. Before that came the intervention of equity. Since a lot of common lawyers think that equity was their idea – and another lot wish that it had never been heard of – we might pause here.

We see equity as softening the hard edges of the law and looking after those who need looking after. Equity also played a large part in Roman law and we might also reflect on what it meant for the Greeks. When we look to the ancient world for law, we look to Rome, not Greece, just as we do in the modern world when we look for opera. The Greeks were keener on theory, and the Romans were keener on practice. But it is sobering to reflect that more than three centuries before the Sermon on the Mount, the Greeks were talking of equity in terms that we now readily recognise.

Aristotle said that all law is universal, but that about some things we cannot make universal statements which will be correct. It is in the nature of equity to be a correction of law where the law is defective owing to its universality. Then a decree is needed, and equity fills the omission of the law. Aristotle went on to say that equity involves forgiveness and considerateness. In his *Rhetoric* (1374b), Aristotle said that equity bids us —

> to settle a dispute by negotiation and not by force; to prefer arbitration to litigation – for an arbitrator goes by the equity of a case, a judge by the law, and arbitration was invented with the express purpose of securing full power for equity.

With Rome, it was the requirements of empire that led to equity. As Rome provided justice not just to Rome, but to all Italy, and beyond, it felt the need to provide its version of the law of nations to the general law by an officer called the *Praetor*. His edicts were sometimes referred to as the law of nature, or the Praetorian law. The process involved a levelling, or a removal of irregularities. The Praetorian law would give rise to claims that we call equitable. Justinian thought he had fused law and equity, and if he was right, he succeeded where we have failed.

At the conclusion of his survey of the phases of development of ancient law, Maine made his famous observation that the movement in progressive societies was a movement from *status* to *contract*. Rather than have their condition set for them from above, by God or a king, people could seek to alter their position by negotiating with and then contracting with other people. This is what some would now call a paradigm shift.

Two things about the practice of the law in Rome. Jurists, the expounders of the law, were more important than judges. There were no professional judges. Judges were appointed annually and were not ordinarily trained lawyers. The body of law called *The Responses of the*

Learned was therefore given by the bar, not by the bench, if for no other reason than there was no bench, at least in the sense that we understand that term.

Another critical difference was that of the two professions in the Republic, the military and the lawyers, the military were the party of movement, and the lawyers were at the head of the party of resistance. In France, the profession tended to side with the Crown. It was not so in England. There the lawyers were normally identified with resistance to the Crown.

We can form some idea of the maturity of the Greek and Roman criminal processes by looking at the two most celebrated criminal trials in history.

Socrates was a Greek philosopher who challenged the establishment and its mode of government. He was charged with worshipping other gods (a charge of blasphemy) and corrupting the youth. The charges were set out in what we would now call written depositions. The case was heard by a council of Athens sitting as a judicial body or as a jury of his neighbours. Socrates cross-examined an accuser and spoke in his own defence. He was found guilty by a very close margin. He could well have avoided death by putting a sensible option which was his right under Athenian law. (Plato was there to be his surety.) But Socrates was driven by his convictions not to take the easy way out. He was sentenced to death after he had said that he would accept freedom of the city and a small fine. It was a painless death in the presence of friends.

We might worry about a charge like corrupting the youth, but is this worse than that of a conspiracy to corrupt public morals which the English judiciary re-invented in the 1960s (*Shaw vDPP*)? All of the ingredients of a fair trial are here – it is far, far in advance of anything in the black hole called Guantanamo Bay.

Jesus was a Palestinian Jew who was a religious teacher. He, too, spoke out against the establishment. He was talked of as being King of the Jews, or the Son of man or the Son of God. (The latter claim would get you executed almost anywhere in the Middle East today.)

There was no written charge but a hearing was held before the High Priest and other functionaries. They appear to have made a finding of blasphemy. They referred the case to Pilate who was the only one empowered to inflict the sentence of death according to the local laws. Pilate put it to Jesus that he called himself the King of the Jews, and this was put on a sign on his place of execution. Pilate was looking for evidence of something like sedition (a false claim to regal power in a Roman province) whereas the provincials were concerned about blasphemy (the admitted claim of the prisoner to be the Son of God).

Jesus in substance refused to plead. Pilate interrogated him. On some accounts in the Gospels, Jesus admitted to claiming to being the Son of God. After Pilate put the issue a number of times, Jesus was convicted. The sentence of death was carried out immediately. This was a revolting exercise in state terror under Roman law (although the law of Moses contemplates death by stoning for some offences).

The problem for us is the confusion over what crime Pilate found Jesus to have committed. It looks like he gave up trying to establish a breach of Roman law and, notwithstanding the sign on the cross, adopted the finding of the local court. Was this trial any less fair or any less of a show trial than the trial that the English gave to Charles I, or that the French gave to Louis Capet?

The thing that impresses us about each of their trials is their speed. We have completely lost the ability to deal expeditiously with trials, either criminal or civil.

But the trial of Jesus gives us hints of why the English may not have accepted Roman law. The hearing before Pilate was a form of inquisitorial process. The contrary would not have been admitted, or even comprehensible to, the Romans. More importantly, torture was used in this proceeding. All four Gospels use the word 'scourge' in the old translations, either in their descriptions of the interrogation or trial, or their record of the prophecy of the fate of Jesus. To 'scourge' a prisoner means to flog, whip or lash him. So John 19.1 reads in the newer translations:

Ancient Law

Then Pilate took Jesus and had him flogged.

In the scale of torture practised by the Romans, a flogging, a possibly lethal punishment which was administered later in the British navy and in penal colonies, may rate at about the level of the waterboarding practised by the US on foreign nationals, but it is very clearly torture. And it was administered not as a punishment – there was then no finding of guilt – but for the purpose associated with its use in the inquisitorial process in Europe – to extract a confession. (According to Acts 22:25, Paul, when taken by the Romans, asked whether it was legal for them to flog a Roman citizen who has not even been found guilty. There are alternative readings in the other gospels that Pilate inflicted torture as part of the final punishment or as a compromise verdict, but torture in the course of the hearing looks more probable.)

The English, at least when their law was as mature as the Roman law applied by Pilate, were never able to accept the use of torture as an instrument of 'justice'. For them, torture and justice is a contradiction in terms. Among other things, it is inarguably against the teaching of the man that the empire of Rome handed over for execution.

This aversion to torture underlay the English distrust of European legal systems, and even today underlies the distrust of English judges and jurists of regimes like Russia and America (although of course the judges are precluded from expressing that distrust in public).

As we shall see, Roman law failed to take hold in England, while it did over the rest of Europe. If we want to find a reason why England is different to the rest of Europe in its laws, here is a place to start. The Latin language was infused into English government and law, and some of its labels and techniques were applied. But this was merely icing on the cake. For the ingredients of the cake itself, we have to look elsewhere.

Although neither Greece nor Rome left any indelible mark on English law, they have had a mixed effect on English political thought. Generations of English lawyers, and other products of Oxford and

Cambridge, have allowed themselves to be deluded into the belief that the societies of Greece and Rome were civilised. Nothing could be further from the truth. Putting to one side that the empire of Rome had through its duly authorised judicial officer ordered the torture and crucifixion of the Saviour of mankind – as the Church of England sees him – Greece and Rome were disqualified from any use of the word 'civilised' that we might now countenance. Athens and Rome at their height ruled and fed off their empires. They also owned and fed off slaves. They legislated and governed by reference to religions which involved a multiplicity of gods that we regard as hopelessly bogus – and indeed whom they found it hard to take seriously. (The one good consequence was that they were tolerant of people who had other religious beliefs.)

The fact that England and indeed Europe could treat these ancient cities and empires as civilised notwithstanding their mortal defects was not good for their moral growth. Nor did it help that the English were invited to subscribe to the view keenly felt both at Athens and at Rome that people who were unable to share the benefits of their world were no better than barbarians.

And it is to one group of those barbarians that we have to look to find the beginnings of English law.

II
The German Influence

But these 600 years are important in our history. They were the years in which England was made by the men of a Teutonic race. They were the years in which these men were converted to Christianity, and admitted thereby to share in the intellectual heritage of the ancient world.

Sir William Holdsworth

I dare not venture to set down in writing much of my own laws, for it was unknown to me what of it would please those who should come after me.

King Alfred the Great

One of the peoples that the Romans derided as barbarians was the German. The leading Roman historian, Tacitus, wrote a book about them (*On Germany*). This is the way he described some of their customs:

> Affairs of the smaller moment the chiefs determine; about matters of higher consequence, the whole nation deliberates.

> In the Assembly, it is allowed to present accusations and to prosecute capital offences. Punishments vary according to the quality of the crime.
>
> Without being armed, they transact nothing, whether of public or private concernment. But it is repugnant to their custom for any man to use arms, before the community has attested his capacity to wield them.
>
> They are almost the only barbarians contented with one wife.
>
> To the husband, the wife tenders no dowry; but the husband to the wife.

There is little that is barbaric here. Indeed, the German view on carrying weapons – essential for such a warlike race – is much more civilised than that adopted by the Supreme Court in the United States in *Heller v District of Columbia*, where the court ruled that every adult in the United States – even an untrained fool – has the right to carry a hand gun, a weapon so much more lethal than anything the barbaric Germans could have dreamed of in their cold, dark woods and bogs.

No, the Roman prejudice was not based on the customs of the kind described by Tacitus, but on the living habits of the Germans, a prejudice carried through to Dante, who in *The Inferno* mocked their consumption of beer, the 'guzzling Germans', and later on the habit of the Germans of defeating the Romans at war.

To understand the common law of England, you have to understand that to the extent that you can talk sensibly of a legal system having roots – either intellectual or ethnic – the roots of English law are German, not Roman. If that proposition sounds large, reflect that we commonly refer to a type of character as 'Anglo Saxon'. By that we mean reticent and matter of fact, as opposed to the flamboyance and symbolism associated with parts of the Continent. The term 'Anglo Saxon' itself derives from the tribes who settled in

The German Influence

England over a period of 600 years or so. Those tribes may not have covered that part of Germany that now produces BMW, but they were identifiably German, and the characteristics that we associate with the phrase Anglo Saxon are among those which distinguish English law from Roman law. Indeed, in some histories you will see the various German settlers described simply as the 'English'.

The Anglo Saxons in England published many codes, and it is now thought that these were free of Celtic or Roman elements. The codes enacted the customary law of the tribe. The Anglo Saxons based their primitive organisation on the ties of kindred, but after the reception of Christianity they were subject to the influence of the church. As Holdsworth remarks, 'the teaching of the church tended to add a new sanctity to the person of the King'.

We get an understanding of how Anglo Saxon law worked in the early Middle Ages from their Charters of Land. The charter ordinarily commences with an invocation 'In the Name of God'. There is then an elaborate form of historical recital, followed by the Grant. Customarily there is a Sanction Clause. These usually consisted of comprehensive curses consigning to damnation, frequently with no lack of gruesome detail, anyone who might attempt to disturb the transaction. There is then the date and signatures. Seals did not come in until other Norman customs were received. Holdsworth remarks that a series of land charters is a unique record of the continuity of Anglo Saxon law 'for they furnished a good root of title to many of the largest estates in medieval England'.

Very early the German tribes provided that wrongs had to be atoned, not merely by compensation to the injured, but by a contribution to the King. We can see here the beginning of a notion of the King's peace. A breach of that peace was an act of personal disobedience, and therefore more serious than other breaches of public order – the wrongdoer was the enemy of the king. In the Anglo-Saxon dooms, homicide can generally be settled by compensation – but not where the killing is in the presence of the king, or otherwise in breach of his peace.

All members of the tribe were obliged to contribute to the militia and in the laws of Aethelbert the neglect of that obligation occupies almost first place. Society was held together by the loyalty owed to the lord and the duty owed to kin. It was 'lifelong infamy' to withdraw from the battle and survive the chief.

As to liability between persons, a man acted at his peril. The primary principle was that an act causing physical damage must, in the interests of peace, be paid for. If you left your arms lying about, and someone else knocked them over so that they killed or hurt a man, you would be liable. If you lent a horse to someone else and the borrower became ill as the result, you would be liable. You had to defend yourself by saying that you had done nothing whereby the other person was 'nearer to death or further from life'. These strict rules have informed the common law on liability for escaping animals or fire to this day. As we shall see, the strict law had its effect on Oliver Wendell Holmes. But someone who is killed by accident or self-defence may be liable to pay the compensation although the wrong itself is atoned for without further punishment.

In those times, the question of ownership of cattle was probably more a live one than the ownership of land. The law did not concern itself so much with ownership as with possession. Even then, it is not so much possession that is protected – what is remedied is an involuntary loss of possession. The law is interested in providing a remedy to someone who has had something in their possession and then lost it. Holmes said this:

> Cattle were the principal property known, and cattle-stealing the principal form of wrongful taking of property. Of law there was very little, and what there was depended almost wholly upon the party himself to enforce. The Salic Law of the fifth century and the Anglo-Saxon laws of Alfred are very full about following the trail.

The German Influence

Just those problems would arise many centuries later in the American West, the Australian bush, and the African veld, but subject to different customary laws, if any.

There was no law of contract as such, but legislators were keen to ensure that transactions were effected before witnesses, or at London. Some arrangements could be settled by a form of homage, one person putting their hands in another's, the remnant of which is shaking hands over a deal.

It is a characteristic feature of the procedural rules of this period of legal history that they are not under the control of the court. They are strict rules that each side must follow and which are designed to produce a result without active intervention by a judge. In a civil suit, the person complaining began by summoning his adversary to the court. There was no specified form under Anglo Saxon law. The summons had to describe the form of action. When served, the other side had then to appear or give an excuse for non-appearance ('essoin'). There was a lot of law about producing the defendant or enforcing his appearance, since there were no police or prisons and the system had to do the work of the policeman, the bail and the prison. But the plaintiff had to produce evidence at the start and swear to the claim and allege it in detail. A similar obligation was on the other side. An explicit denial was called for: 'In the name of the living God, I owe not to John one shilling, or penny or penny's worth; but I have discharged to him all that I owe him, so far as our verbal contracts were at first.' There is a fore-runner of our idea of onus in the German attraction to the principle that 'denial is always stronger than accusation'.

The person who made the proof won the case. The procedure for the most part was not concerned with the merits. This would come in later when the jury was introduced. Most people find litigation an ordeal. The Germans literally imposed an ordeal as a mode of proof. You could plunge your hand into burning water and take out a stone. If your hand healed after three days, you were cleared. This was the judgment of God.

But the more general mode was by oath. The oath did not go to a specific issue of fact, but to the justice of the claim or defence over all. If the oath was made according to form, it was conclusive. What we call the burden was for the old Germans a benefit. It is not until the jury determines issues of fact on the evidence that the process of trial is moved from the supernatural in the direction of the rational.

III
The French Connection

The polite luxury of the Norman presented a striking contrast to the coarse voracity and drunkenness of his Saxon and Danish neighbours...During the century and a half which followed the Conquest, there is, to speak strictly, no English history.
> *Macaulay*

We were not born to sue but to command.
...
There shall your swords and lances arbitrate
The swelling difference of your settled hate
Since we cannot atone you, we shall see
Justice design the victor's chivalry.
> *Richard II*

Everyone knows what a writ is. Someone is unhappy about what someone else has done. They want to refer the dispute to court. For that purpose, they ask the court to issue a document which will be served on the other side, requiring them to attend court and answer their complaint. That is a writ, and this chapter is about writs.

We are at the time that is the subject of the work of Pollock & Maitland, *The History of English Law before the time of Edward I*, a work of two volumes published in 1899, a work of immense scholarship of the kind hardly seen now. (It will be here referred to as Maitland, because he wrote almost all of it except for the part on Anglo-Saxon law.) Maitland said of this time, 'The rule of law was the rule of writs'.

Since we are talking of the Middle Ages, it is as well to remember the influence of God and his church. Holdsworth referred to the dry remark of one scholar:

> The word Churchman means today one who belongs to the Church as against others. In the Middle Ages, there were no others, or, if there were, they were occupied in being burnt.

In such a religious era, the resolution of questions of both law and fact was likely to be seen as in the province of God, and the history of the common law is in some part a history of the shift of judicial jurisdiction from God and his church to people.

It was also an age of primitive customs and self-help. In some cases of crime, where a thief was caught red-handed, the accused could be dealt with on the spot and 'properly hanged, beheaded or precipitated from a cliff, and the owner of the stolen goods will perhaps act as an amateur executioner'. As Maitland remarked, criminals of those times were most likely to dread the justice of 'the kind which we now associate with the name of Mr. Lynch'. The Normans, like their German predecessors and like their American successors, went armed. But, and perhaps because of this, professional lawyers were not yet on the scene.

The Normans spoke French but derived from the north of Europe, a part not terribly far away from where the Germans had come. There is no doubt that their hold on England was firm after the Conquest. Maitland thought that the process we are about to see was made possible by 'the exceptional vigour of the English kingship' and 'the exceptional malleableness was of a thoroughly conquered and compactly united kingdom'.

What we are looking at is the tendency of the English law to start with a form of remedy – a form of writ – and then later develop a body of law to support it. This is fundamentally different to the Roman law

The French Connection

model, of a code or body of law that is looked to in order to see what procedure should be followed. Nowadays we have a general procedure and there are very few specific procedures. The special procedure in Admiralty is one exception. In the period we are looking at, it is hard to discern any general form of process, but rather we are looking at what might happen under any number of writs.

The English were following the earlier German precedents that classified their form of proceeding (or action) according to the relief that was sought from the court, rather than the legal right that was being invoked. It was in this period that we get the first textbook of the common law. It is called, usually, Glanvill, although it can be entitled *The Laws and Customs of England*. Glanvill occupied the office of Justiciar, or Justice, in the reigns of Henry II and Richard I. He was not however a professional lawyer. His book, translated, occupies less than 180 pages. It is a paradigm textbook of English law – it consists of precedents, mainly writs, and some short discussion of them with little or no analysis or theory. Here is the first precedent and therefore the first recorded precedent of the common law. 'A writ for making the first summons':

> The King to the Sheriff, Greetings. Command N to render to R justly and without delay [acre] of land and such a vill[age] which the said R complains that the said N is withholding from him. If he does not do so, summon him by good summoners to be before me or my justices on the day after the eighth of Easter to show why he has not done so. And have there the summons and this writ. Witness Rannul Glanvill, at Clarendon.

Would that other precedents were as simple and to the point as this – the first. Glanvill's discussion of the causes of indebtedness occupies about a page.

Here is the form for a 'plea' of the crime of rape.

> The crime of rape, a woman charges a man with violating her by force in the peace of the Lord King. A woman who suffers

in this way must go, soon after the deed is done, to the nearest vill[age] and there show to trustworthy men the injury done to her, and any effusion of blood there may be and any tearing of her clothes. She should then do the same to the [sheriff] of the [neighbourhood].

The law at this time knew no difference between civil claims and criminal claims or pleas. By and large, each cause for what we would call a civil action constituted what we would call an offence, and every cause for a civil action in the court of the King was an offence against the King, punishable according to the rules of the time. The proceeding instituted in respect of the more serious crimes was then called an appeal. But, as we will see, an action for trespass was closely related to the appeal of a crime.

A person wanting to go to court went to the Chancery, the registry of the court, and obtained a writ, by paying for it. The Chancellor at this time has not heard the story of the defendant, and the function of the writ, as we can see from that given by Glanvill above, was to get the other side before the court. The law then continues to be preoccupied with that function and for a long, long time declined to give judgment against someone who had not appeared. The ultimate sanction against the reluctant defendant was outlawry, which involved a sentence of death.

The law of arrest was then very crude. (It has not got much better since – a standard American Bar Association text, *Arrest: The Decision to Take a Suspect into Custody,* runs for 540 pages.) There might be a trial by battle or by ordeal. These might be said to involve the supernatural – the fiction was that what triumphed in battle was not brute force but the truth – but the supernatural is invoked every day in our courts when someone is asked to take the oath, just as it was in those days when the mode of trial was whether a person could get a sufficient number of people to swear to their credibility.

The person starting the proceeding had to produce a 'suit' of witnesses. For crimes that were appealed, the person bringing the appeal had to provide 'proof by his body'. No one was entitled to begin a proceeding with nothing but a bare assertion – what was then called *nude parole*. The role of the court was then seen to be simply to fix the mode of proof and then see which side prevailed according to the mechanism of proof. The court was not then inclined to weigh conflicting testimonies.

The Normans brought with them the use of the inquisition in public administration – the practice of ascertaining facts by summoning people competent as neighbours to know the answer. This practice fitted well with the Anglo-Saxon tradition of popular justice – their old courts were a 'sort of town-meeting of judges'. But gradually the jury, originally a form of inquiry or inquisition by those who might be thought to have had the answers, became an attractive way of trying issues of fact.

A jury trial might be attractive to both sides in view of the grisly consequences of drawing the short straw under the archaic modes of battle, ordeal, or multiple swearings. For example, in trial by battle the person carrying the onus lost 'if the stars appeared before the fight was over' (which would have made unsettling reading if the fight had started before lunch).

The significance of the advent of the jury as a finder of fact is described by Professor Milsom in his introduction to the reissue of Pollock & Maitland as follows:

> Substantive law is the product of thinking about facts. What takes a legal system beyond the mere classification of claims is the adoption of a mode of trial which allows the facts to come out. In England, the starting point was the introduction of jury processes …The intellectual beginnings of the common law are epitomised in a manuscript which … ends as a Year Book … We can see the introduction of a rational trial as the opening of a door which led out into a modern world.

In truth, the jury was to become what Blackstone called 'the principal criterion of truth in the law of England'.

Common Law

The King liked the new forms of procedure. This was a royal commodity and he could sell it. Since the King was interested in all breaches of the King's peace, which we shall come back to, he would prefer a form of inquest than to chance his arm on the arm of the person complaining, who may not be in the same league as the other side who is presumably described as a wicked criminal.

By the time of Bracton, the right of the person challenged 'to put himself upon his country for good and ill' was accepted. We have come to the point where jurors are not witnesses, but judges of fact. And the court sees the verdict as the verdict of the country. 'Justices seem to feel that if they analyse the verdict they would miss the very thing for which they are looking, the opinion of the country'. More importantly, the jury was at the heart of a system of justice that was at once popular and public.

So we have a law common to England, being the writ of the royal court that runs throughout the realm, but we also have the beginning of the common law as we understand that term, a law made up by decisions of the courts. Decision or decree in one case becomes a guide, if not a rule, for a decision in a later case. The custom of the court passes into law. The question of 'What should we do now?' invites the question: 'What have we done in the past?'

The following words of Maitland are fundamental to our understanding of our law, both then and now:

> The behaviour which is expected of a judge in different ages and by different systems of law seems to fluctuate between two poles. As one of these the model is the conduct of the man of science who is making researches in his laboratory and will use all appropriate methods for the solution of problems and the discovery of truth. At the other stands the umpire of our English games, who is there, not in order that he may invent tests for the powers of the two sides, but simply to see that the rules of the game are observed. It is towards the second of these ideals that our English medieval procedure is strongly inclined. We are often reminded of the cricket match. The judges sit in

court, not in order that they may discover the truth, but in order that they may answer the question. 'How's that?' ... But even in a criminal cause, even when the King is prosecuting, the English judge will, if he can, play the umpire rather than the inquisitor.

These thoughts are fundamental to us still. The comparison with the man of science is precisely what Oliver Wendell Holmes had in mind when he made his famous observation that 'The life of the law has not been logic, it has been experience'. This is apparent from his later observation that 'as the law is administered by able and experienced men, who know too much to sacrifice good sense to a syllogism ...' The concluding distinction between the common law judge and the inquisitor shows that the English have now clearly rejected the Roman law model.

Maitland, and it must be said Pollock also, did not disguise their relief. They referred to the new procedures for the inquisition introduced by Innocent III. They said that the safeguards of innocence were disregarded and that torture was freely used, to the point that 'the common law of Western Europe adopted it'. Because, they said, the English system had not gone down the way of the Inquisition, England had avoided the impulse that 'might have sent it down that too easy path which the Church chose and which led to the everlasting bonfire'.

We will have to come back to this subject of torture, because its judicial damnation is one of the singular triumphs of the common law of England. We note here simply that Pollock and Maitland referred to the 'escape of the English from secrecy and torture' and said that the use of torture had involved 'half proof' by the confession of the accused, a 'cruel and stupid subterfuge'. Their conclusion was that English law had emancipated itself 'from the old formulated oaths, and it trusted for a while to the rough verdicts of the countryside, without caring to investigate the logical proccsses, if logical they were, of which that verdict was the outcome'.

Common Law

The King who championed royal justice over local and feudal courts was Henry II. He deserves to be remembered as the father of the common law, but he is remembered as the murderer in the cathedral. This was one of those conflicts between the royal and the ecclesiastical powers, dominions, and principalities that have – for better or for worse – shaped the English character and law.

IV
The Great Charter

Mad world, mad kings, mad composition!
(The Bastard in *King John*)

King John did not sign Magna Carta;
there is no evidence that he could write.
(Holt)

In the play *King John*, the Bastard laments 'that smooth faced gentleman, tickling commodity…the bias of the world' (2.1.583-4). Greed was lord of all; everything was up for grabs. John was to find that loyalty – the fealty of his subjects, especially the barons – was up for grabs. He would have to buy it.

Tax and overseas military service are potent sources of tension that can bring down a crown. Frequently the two combine when the crown has to increase its taxes to fund a war. John got into trouble with his barons on both counts. The English was not the only feudal aristocracy to react against a demand for military service outside the realm.

There were, as we would now say, other issues. Justice was a commodity, bought and sold like any other commodity. Justice was the King's or the Lord's to dispense – and take profit from. Glanvill saw the institution of a jury trial 'as a royal favour bestowed on the people by the clemency of the Prince on the advice of his magnates'. This had to be paid for, as did other exercises of royal grace. This led to a form of proffer – an open offer, an offer that was open to competitors to beat. It would be like buying writs today on e-Bay. Bids of five marks or one palfrey were common. It was suggested that those who lost their case might get lenient treatment on recovery of the amount proffered. This, predictably, led to a form of contingent fee, a proffer based on success.

These were hard and rough times. The barons might resemble either Mafia Dons or Jihadists, depending on your taste – whether you see the exercise as one involving terrorism is little more than a matter of taste. One of their leaders, Robert fitz Walter styled himself 'Marshall of the Army of God and Holy Church'. The law itself was violent and relied on violence for its execution; officers of the king were liable in their bodies for the conduct of their offices. One of the 25 barons appointed under the Charter, Robert de Ros, was a marauding land rustler whose men attacked agents of the Sheriff of Yorkshire with bows and arrows. (King John, we are told, had at least five bastards, but took a bath once every three weeks.)

The barons arrived at Runnymede armed. In truth, the nation was embroiled in a civil war, although this in the Charter was spun down to 'discord'. But King John could not afford to take the fatuous position that he would not negotiate with terrorists. The barons had withdrawn, expressly, their fealty, and they were involved in passive disobedience before it descended into war. The document *Magna Carta* was not signed by the King. It took effect when it was sealed by an oath, a sanction that had more power then than now. The King almost immediately set about trying to repudiate the document by alleging duress to the Pope.

The document does have signs of duress. We will look at the sanctions clause (Article 61), but Article 55 deals with the remission of fines made 'unjustly and contrary to the law of the land'. It is almost impossible to get a CEO or government minister to admit having acted either unjustly or, unlawfully, and it must have been

The Great Charter

just as hard to get such an admission from God's anointed, even at the point of a sword.

As a medieval document sworn to in Christendom, the Charter began and ended with references to God. But worryingly for Rome, the church is the Church of England and the Charter expressly says, twice, that the 'English Church shall be free'.

The barons were too smart to make themselves the only beneficiaries of their negotiations with the King. The vindication of the Church may or may not have been a veneer, but the class of beneficiaries of the Charter is wide. There is relief for guardians, wards, and widows. 'No widow shall be compelled to marry so long as she wishes to live without a husband'. Debts to the Jews and the ancient liberties of London are provided for. There is to be a standing court for ordinary civil actions. Extensive provisions deal with fines and legal process.

The most famous parts are clauses 39 and 40:

> 39. No free man shall be taken or imprisoned or diseised or outlawed or exiled or in any way ruined, nor will be go or send against him, except by the lawful judgment of his peers or by the law of the land.
>
> 40. To no one will we sell, to none will we deny or delay right or justice.

These clauses are pleasingly plastic enough to enable future development. As one example, what does the 'or' signify towards the end of clause 39 – indeed, is 'or' the correct translation? – or is clause 40 in such broad terms that it has been and continues to be violated on a daily basis by every court in the common law world?

We saw that Anglo Saxon charters had a form of sanction that resembled a curse. Article 61 resembles something far more specific – it is like the power to appoint a receiver given by someone issuing a debenture to secure the repayment of money. It did not reappear in the later editions – it was, in truth, a licence to commit treason that could only effectively be exercised in what would otherwise be an act of civil war. The sanction clause shows the malignance of the King and the complete lack of trust in him by the barons. If there is a default on the part of the King, the 25 nominated barons can seize royal property. Finally they are to act with the 'commune' of the whole land. This takes us forward to the French Revolution and the other revolutions in Europe in the middle of the century after that revolution. The barons have a licence to get the whole of the people to join in resisting a recalcitrant Crown. It is a standing threat of civil war – or, more correctly, a threat to restart the civil war that this treaty was supposed to end. It matters not that the barons were over-mighty, self-centred thugs. What revolution was won by the meek?

At about the time of *Magna Carta,* the Hungarians agreed to what was called *The Golden Bull* and the Spaniards agreed to a *Privilegio de la Union*, but neither achieved the standing of *Magna Carta* or anything like it. Sir James Holt summarised the legal result of *Magna Carta* as follows:

> Magna Carta accepted and took over practically all the judicial
> procedures of Henry II, whether King John liked it or not.
> And in such processes several changes occurred. The Crown's
> routine convenience was converted into the subjects' customary
> rights; procedure and routine process were used to manufacture
> substantive law, a transmutation which quickened once men
> had begun, as Glanvill had, to compare English custom with
> the Roman Leges; and custom, about which the Crown and its
> subjects might argue, was converted into statute which brooked no
> debate… It was just this which Magna Carta achieved.

William Stubbs has been criticised for romancing about the Charter, but he was plainly right when he said that the 'whole of the constitutional history of England is a commentary on this charter'. He might have said the same for what we now call administrative law. As the document came to be reissued, it was not long before the phrase 'due process of law' was invoked, and that takes us to natural justice and procedural fairness, and to the fourth and fourteenth amendments to the Bill of Rights in the US.

Maitland was enough of an English lawyer – he read at the bar in a conveyancer's chambers – to realise that the very definite promises about smaller matters were perhaps of greater value than some of the more windy suspirations. Those provisions could be enforced as law in courts of law – the courts could hardly enforce against the King his covenant that he would not sell or deny justice, or that he would appoint as judges only those who know the law (another provision of our law which is breached on a daily basis). He said that:

> with all its faults, the document had become a kind of 'sacred text', the nearest approach to an irrepealable 'fundamental' statute that England has ever had ... For in brief it means this, that the King is and shall be below the law.

And although clause 39 may not have had much immediate effect on private rights, its constitutional significance is immense. It came to be seen as laying down the principle that liberty and property are not to be taken away without 'due process'.

It is easy to state and difficult to over-emphasize the importance of *Magna Carta*. It has that quality most loved by common lawyers. It is a precedent. It is a precedent for restraining an abuse of power. The Charter is as important for the fact that it was created as for what it said. It showed that the King could be made to answer or, in the awful language of today, that the King was accountable. The King had had to come to the table and deal. He had had to negotiate with his people on the terms on which they would allow him to continue to hold the Crown and give him their loyalty. He had had to be negotiable.

After nearly four centuries had elapsed, another King would find that not even God could save his crown or his head if he declared himself to be non-negotiable to his people. We have seen that Maine saw the movement of progressive societies as being from status to contract. We usually see this movement among the subjects of the Crown, but now we can see it with the Crown itself. It has begun to move from its status as having been appointed from above by God – the Divine Right of Kings – to where the crown depends on the terms of the compact between the holder of the crown and its subjects. The movement is from status to contract.

Although he sought to renege immediately, King John had bought some time for the crown. That nearly eight centuries have since elapsed suggests that the deal was not such a bad one for either the Crown or for the people of England. But, however that may be, after 1215, a claim of divine right by any king would have the same intellectual value as a claim that the sun revolved around the earth.

Both sides to the civil war had had to yield to the Pope as a kind of feudal superior. John sought to have the deal quashed by the Pope on the ground of duress. The barons had given primacy to the right of the English church to be free. There might obviously come a time when the English dealing with their Crown would not want to be second guessed by someone claiming a higher source of power. It is not much good getting rid of a claim to divine right if it can be reinvested by a foreign power.

By the time that Shakespeare wrote, the conflict between the English crown and the Church of Rome had been resolved, adversely to Rome. Shakespeare put into the mouth of King John the following rebuff to the Pope.

> What earthy name to interrogatories
> Can test the free breath of a sacred King?
> …
> Tell him this tale, and from the mouth of England
> Add thus much more that no Italian priest
> Shall tide or toll in our dominions:
> But as we, under Heaven, are supreme head.
> So, under him, that great supremacy. (3.1, 74–83)

The Great Charter

Those words to this day can get a warmish response from an English audience, although, in fairness to the author, he was very generous in a later play in his treatment of the first innocent victim of Henry VIII, Catherine of Arragon – and if John had had the force of character of Henry, as well his downright nastiness, the constitution may have taken much longer to take shape.

In the same century as *Magna Carta*, there appeared the second great text of English law. We call it Bracton, *On the Laws and Customs of England.* Its origins are medievally obscure. Like most 'judges' of the time, Bracton had taken Holy Orders. He served on the King's Court. The book is in four volumes. In the current reprint of the Thorne Edition, itself a monument to American scholarship, it covers 25 centimetres on the shelf. Although Bracton took a lot from Roman law, he sought to expound the whole of English law rationally, something not often attempted, let alone achieved. Maitland called it the 'crown and flower' of English jurisprudence. 'Romanesque in form, English in substance'; it expressly cites some 500 cases. It achieved a kind of veneration as a sponsor of a constitutional monarchy.

> The king is below no man, but he is below God and the law; law makes the king; the king is bound to obey the law …

We must now look at the most prominent schizoid break in the law – the split between law and morals, between law and equity.

V
The Growth of Equity

A perfectly simple principle can never be applied to a state of things which is the reverse of simple.

Plato, The Statesman

The clerical chancellors were exercising the temporal counterpart of the confessional.

J.H. Baker

We saw earlier that Greek philosophy and Roman law had developed the notion of equity. Because no lawmaker can envisage every case that may arise, the law needs to reserve some elastic for itself. If you try to force everyone on to the bed of Procrustes great unhappiness will arise. But, if too much elastic is allowed, the law may descend into a lottery. You can try to mask this to some extent by distinguishing between written and unwritten law – although some take the view that there can be no such thing as an unwritten law – but ultimately you will come up with a proposition to the effect that the supplement to the law, the equitable supplement, should be in the spirit of the law itself, or follow the law, or do what the law would have done if it had envisaged the particular case.

Before looking at the rise of equity in England, we might reflect on the huge contribution that equity made to Roman law, and now makes to European law. Those contributions, apart from the triumph of the nature of the blood relationship, were summarised by Sir Carleton Allen as follows.

It was Roman equity that led to the principle of good faith in contractual obligations. This is a major distinction between European laws and the common law. The Roman Praetor adopted as a dogma of interpretation that wherever possible the intention rather than the form should be looked to. Roman law had a more comprehensive prohibition of unjust enrichment at the expense of another and had developed it to an extent which has only recently been matched, if at all, by the common law. If, under this Roman law, you came into possession of property not your own, even though by accident or mistake, and without deliberate fraud, you had a strict obligation to return the property or its value to the true owner.

Perhaps the most distinctive contribution of Roman equity to our eyes now was in its opposition to what we may well now call subtlety (the Latin was *subtilitas*) – the adherence to the strict letter of the law in order to make it the means of unscrupulous advantage. As Allen observed, 'the essence of the wrong complained of is not that it is illegal, but that it is too legal'. This, in turn, leads to the principle of *abuse of right*, which is referred to in some modern European systems as *chicane*. Any law that looks askance at subtlety has every chance of being a very good law. (Counsel knows that they have lost the judge when their argument is called 'ingenious' or, worse, 'clever'.)

Before the development of English equity in Chancery, research now shows that English people sought what we would call equity from the travelling justices by documents that were simply in the nature of 'bills'. These prayed for a remedy 'for God's sake', 'for charity's sake', or 'for love of Jesus Christ'. They required a different kind of drafting to the later equity documents. Here is how one proceeded:

> Dear Sir, of you who are put in the place of Our Lord the King to do right to poor and rich.

> I cry mercy, I John – make my complaint to God and you, Sir Justice, that Richard the carpenter…detains from me six marks which I paid him upon receiving from him an undertaking in writing by which he bound himself to find me in board and lodging in return for the money … And for this I cry you mercy, dear Sir, and pray, for God's sake, that you will see that I get my money back before you leave this town…As soon, my Lord, I get my money I shall go to the Holy Land and there I will pray for the King of England and for you…For I tell you that not a farthing I have to spend on a pleader; and so for this, dear Sir, be gracious to me that I may get me my money back.

Maitland commented on this ancient royal equity that it could be invoked to 'defeat the devices of those who would use legal forms for the purpose of chicane', surely an unconscious reference by Maitland to the Roman law.

There is nothing about equity being administered by the Chancery in Glanvill or Bracton, but the equity function of the court of Chancery was proceeding by the time of Richard II. Bracton was content to suppose that where people had to complain of the inadequacy of the common law to the King in his Council, the complaint was referred to the Chancellor. A Chancellor under Richard II developed a writ to compel the attendance of a person who, it was alleged, had been abusing a trust (the person we sometimes call a fiduciary). The writ had to be obeyed on pain of penalty (*sub poena*).

The Chancery began as the royal secretariat. The Chancellor kept the royal seal and had a large staff of clerks. The Chancellors were frequently church people, who were *de facto* Prime Ministers – such as Cardinal Wolsey. But above the Chancellor, the Anglo Saxon and early Norman and English Kings were said to be 'fountains of justice' and, to this day, the English Crown retains a prerogative of mercy, if not equity. Trusts were not binding at common law, but were said to be binding in conscience by the clergy, who, as we have seen, supplied the personnel for the Chancery.

The Growth of Equity

Justice Story thought that the initial petitions were in respect of outrages like assaults that could as a matter of form be dealt with at common law, but where the adversary had 'protection' by a powerful baron or sheriff. Story said that:

> It was not abuse of patron for the purpose of acquiring and exercising ownership; but a beneficial interposition, to correct gross injustice and to redress aggravated and intolerable grievances.

Proceedings were supposed to be informal. There was no writ, but just a document called a bill, usually in English.

While Wolsey, More and Bacon played prominent parts in the development of the office, two of those were appallingly corrupt, and the other was executed in the course of the religious power struggles. The great legal expounders of this law, if that is an appropriate description, were Lords Nottingham and Hardwicke.

We get an idea of how equity operated from a case on a bond. A man bound himself to pay a certain sum of money on a certain day. He went overseas and left his wife to deliver the documents. She failed to do so. He is not therefore able to deny that he did not tender the document on the day fixed. But he says that the person complaining has suffered no damage. That person, like Shylock, relies on the words of the bond. The court ruled that the plaintiff was not seeking to recover a debt but a penalty. 'What equity would it be to award you the debt when the document is tendered and you cannot show that you have been damaged by the detention?' The plaintiff was then told he would have to wait for seven years for his judgment.

But the rise of the Chancery led to the conflict with the common law judges. Judges are supposed to end conflict, not start it. Wolsey was a slippery bureaucrat with no academic training, who delighted in putting lawyers down. His successor, the saintly Sir Thomas More, understood the problem but told the common law judges over dinner that they could be a little less rigorous. This did not help them. A while later, Lord Ellesmere granted lots of injunctions to stop common law process and then outraged the common lawyers even more by appointing as Master of the Rolls a Doctor of Civil Law with the modest name of Sir Julius Caesar. One of the things that rightly troubles litigants is the sight of divided counsels and the sound of warring judges. It was to continue with Coke and Bacon.

The doctrine relied on by equity was that of *conscience* and statutory invocations of it nowadays frequently talk of *unconscionable* conduct. It was expounded in a treatise called St Germain, *Doctor and Student*. A doctor of divinity who does not understand the technical rules of law seeks enlightenment from a student of law about the attitude of our law towards conscience and he is told, among other things, that 'the extreme righteousness is extreme wrong: as who says, if you take all that the words of the law give you, you shall sometimes do against the law'.

Some people get nervous at the thought that law might enforce morals. You might be able to take morals out of malice in the criminal law, or perhaps the law of libel, but surely not from the law of theft, which involves taking something that does not belong to you dishonestly. Or the law of equity, which stops people acting against good conscience. What is the difference between acting dishonestly or against good conscience on the one hand, and acting immorally on the other?

Sir Thomas More said that equity was concerned with 'fraud, accident, and things of confidence'. 'Things of confidence' include trusts, the equity of redemption under a mortgage, the obligations that we now categorise as fiduciary, or obligations of integrity between people such as partners or lawyers and their clients. When equity referred to *fraud* it was talking about unconscionable dealing short of deceit at common law. The doctrine of accident has not been substantially developed. Equity also had jurisdiction in respect of infants, married women and others who were subject to a disability, including at one time the poor and the insane, and objects of charity generally.

With time equity hardened by its own precedents and the rigour of the law was topped by the rigour of equity. You can find an underlying sense of intellectual and moral superiority in a lot of pronouncements of Chancery that led to its being too pure for its own purposes. It became mired in frightful doctrinal formulations and procedural difficulties, and was one of the chief targets of Charles Dickens in *Bleak House*.

In many ways Dickens let them off too lightly. The landed families of England were fortunate if they were not looted by lawyers from Chancery at some time or other. By the 18th century, the backlog was about 20,000 and some causes were still not determined after thirty years. Two distinguished Chancellors were dismissed for accepting 'presents'. Masterships were sold for the fantastic price of £5,000. Some of the tricks of judges and lawyers have an alarmingly modern aroma. Since every step in litigation attracted fees, there was no incentive for expedition or finality. Reports were lengthened by multiple recitals. Sixty clerks were paid by the page – and lo! their handwriting got bigger and their margins got wider. Just think what these clerks could have done with a good photocopier and computer.

As an example of a law that became a victim of its own inbreeding, the law of charity still, at least at what we call common law, turns on determining whether or not the relevant trust may be said to be informed by a purpose that is within 'the spirit and intendment' of the preamble to a statute of Queen Elizabeth – not the present Queen Elizabeth, but Elizabeth I. The most frightful esoteric learning can then arise, which can have singular effects on whether a person's property dispositions are to take effect, and it may also have very significant effects on the revenue. Some of the case law – and it used to be both voluminous and impenetrable – is disconcerting. For example, trusts for 'the prayer, contemplation, penance and self-sanctification' of an order of cloistered nuns were held not to be charitable (*Gilmour v Coats*) but a bequest 'for the welfare of cats and kittens needing care and attention' was upheld as serving a good charitable purpose by being 'calculated to develop the finer side of human nature' (*Re Moss*). To enter on to one of these cases for the first time and to hear counsel expound the law is like landing on the moon.

Equity was involved in new remedies. We saw that the writ of covenant gave a form of what we call an order for specific performance, but this remedy is – still – associated with equity. The Chancellor restrained abuses of conscience in common proceedings by issuing an injunction. The writ of subpoena was used to get people before the court.

Other additions have turned sour. As Story remarked, every proceeding in Chancery was like a claim (or suit) for discovery, since the defendants were required to go on oath to give an account of their conduct. Here we have the opposite of the criminal procedure. The Chancellor never had a jury to settle issues of fact. Evidence was taken by sworn statements (affidavits). Perhaps the distant and aloof other-worldliness of Chancery would not have been so bad if its judges had been brought back to earth by a jury now and then. That is of course one of the great untouted functions of the jury – to keep the bench in touch with the rest of us, even if it is not part of us.

Discovery and written witness statements are two of the great scandals of our current procedure. Discovery descends into paper warfare to the grim but grateful benefit of those lawyers who charge by the hour and have nothing better to do with their very modest talents. The concoction of written witness statements leads to orchestrations of misleading evidence that mock the notion that a witness must tell nothing but the truth and that their lawyers are not there to give evidence. These fabrications lead inevitably to statements that are downright false. It is sad to see how appalled honest people are when told they have to participate in a process that seems to them to have been devised for the enrichment of lawyers and the burial of the truth. If the Chancery was created to protect the poor and the innocent, its processes are now routinely used or abused to protect the rich and the guilty. Every day, the ceremony of innocence is drowned, with the other consequences foreseen by the poet.

The inevitable tension in any legal system between having too little leeway and too much was set out with precision about 2,000 years ago by a Roman orator, Quintilian:

The Growth of Equity

> There is a tribe of ingenious pleaders who would have us 'interpret' this statute. It does not, they claim, mean what it says. I greatly admire the subtlety of these advocates: they are much more acute than our ancestors – those mere founders of the law, mere framers of our legal system: they must be more acute, or they would not attempt to show that these ancestors of ours lacked both speech and sense. ... If the court is always to be spending its time turning statutes inside out to discover what is just and what is equitable and what is expedient: well, then, there might as well be no statutes at all. No doubt there was a time when law was nothing but a kind of native justice ... We might just as well have no laws at all as uncertain laws.

An element of moral superiority seems to follow equity lawyers – sometimes called 'whisperers'. Maitland remarked that a system that sent every question of fact to a jury was not competent to deal adequately with fiduciary relationships. Why on earth not? A fiduciary, the most abused word in our law, is simply someone in a position of trust. The people on the street know as much about that as the people off the street. Why should not a jury answer questions about whether someone has been trustworthy when on a daily basis they answer questions about whether people have been careless or dishonest or motivated by what the law calls malice?

It is not that a fiduciary has to be honest. We all have to be. Rather, a person in a position of trust may have more duties of honesty – or, if you prefer, integrity – just because other people have put trust in them. Honesty between a barrister and client may involve more than honesty between a Jermyn Street shop as retailer and the barrister as shopper, but you do the law a great wrong to say that there should be a different source of law or a different kind of court to rule on whether the impugned conduct deserves to be adjudged dishonest.

In the reign of Queen Victoria, the English passed legislation to fuse law and equity. To the eyes of the untutored observer, the plain object of the law could be described as 'seeing the old whore churched at last'. To its continuing shame, the common law is still up in the air about what this 'fusion' means. This is not an argument proper for the common law, but one for medieval Schoolmen debating how many angels can dance on the point of a needle.

We see here another problem with the practice of equity in some jurisdictions. Allied to a sense of moral superiority, you may find a certain intellectual smugness. This can find expression in a kind of elevated refinement and an adherence to form and a horror of innovation. This attitude was typified in the last century in England by Lord Simonds, a man of vast learning and refinement whose puritanical rigidity caused even Parliament to intervene on the side of humanity. The jurisdiction that was developed to be informal and to help the poor to deal with the rigour of the law had well and truly devoured itself. This frequently happens with revolutions.

VI
A Profession for Lawyers

The education, the discipline, the whole life of the Inns of Court was collegiate in the best sense of the word ... There will be perhaps, some danger that the law thus technically learned will become more and more esoteric; and that appreciation will develop into an uncritical complacency. But this mode of training will ... maintain in the common law and the common lawyers that boldness in the face of authority which has always been the chief bulwark of our constitutional liberties.

Holdsworth

From 1290 to 1310 there was a very brilliant Bar in England.

Theodore Plucknett

We are seeing the common law develop in the hands of the legal profession of England. Since, as we shall see, the constitution of England is part of the common law, we should look at those who have developed this profession and constitution.

The Romans, but not the Anglo Saxons, allowed people to plead cases for others. This course does, after all, call for a relationship of agency – Peter has to be able to speak on behalf of John. By the time of Edward I, there was in England a legal profession of sorts – a class of people who represented others or gave advice for a fee. Prior to then, people had been allowed to take friends to court and take 'counsel' with them, as happens now in some jurisdictions for litigants who are indigenous or poor. When the system got under way, one advantage for the litigant may have been deniability, the deniability that government ministers now seek from their spokesmen. A pleader did not have the authority of an attorney – an attorney had been appointed or attorned, that is, 'turned to the business in hand'.

The earliest pleaders were an uncomely assembly of 'countors' and those brought up in Roman or canon law. They were not experts in English law. But by the time of Edward I, the split in the English profession had taken place. The spread was between pleaders, who went to court, and attorneys, who acted more generally. And some control was being exercised already in the 13th century, some of it looking ahead to our times. 'The civic fathers were further compelled to threaten with suspension the pleader who took money with both hands or reviled his antagonist.' At the beginning, the only training was on the job – in court – and the opinion of those at the bar was as weighty as the judgments of the bench.

The practice of the law became a profession when those we now know as barristers formed colleges that were known then and now as Inns of Court. Before looking at them, we might notice a textbook from these times, our third. It is Sir John Fortescue's *In Praise of the Laws of England*. Fortescue was prominent in the times of Henry VI, politically and legally. He progressed through the ranks of King's Serjeant to the bench. His book continues the theme of parliamentary monarchy. It also gives the earliest picture of the Inns of Court and the profession.

Edward I, the English Justinian, directed the judges to make provision for the apprentices of the law. (Apprentice comes from *apprendre*, to learn.) The apprentices were trained in the Inns of Court – Lincoln's, Gray's, and the Inner and Middle Temple. Oxford and Cambridge taught Roman and canon law; the Inns taught English law.

The origins of the Inns were and are obscure, even for Fortescue, but we do know that the Temple came from property originally held by the Order of the Templars, and then the Hospitallers. It seems that these societies developed from places for accommodation (inns) for lawyers attending courts in London, just as Lloyd's insurers take their name from the coffee shop in London where the underwriters first met. The inns were controlled by the Benchers (normally judges) who acted like Fellows at the colleges of Oxford and Cambridge. These inns were to be the university of the common law for centuries.

Teaching consisted of lectures and arguments. It was much, much more practical – experiential, if you like – than what law schools at universities offer law students now. A senior reader would read some act or precedent and it would then be argued by the apprentice barristers in order of their degree. In term time cases were argued after dinner, and moots were held after supper; even in what were called the 'dead vacations' the same course was followed with Utter Barristers taking the place of the Benchers. Following Maitland, Holdsworth said that 'law schools conducted after this fashion made "tough law".' Maitland said:

> Now it would, so I think, be difficult to conceive any scheme better suited to harden and toughen a traditional body of law than one which, while books were still uncommon, compelled every lawyer to take part in legal education, and every distinguished lawyer to read public lectures.

Procedure was always to the fore, and you wonder if they ever found time or taste for theory. The readings and moots could be cited in arguments in the courts. It was a mode of instruction that began by making men pleaders – there were of course no women, or men from the lower orders, at first – it kept them going as debaters and advocates, and finished with them as judges. It gave us the men who gave us the Year Books. It was a form of higher education claimed by the privileged whether they intended to practise law or not, and to that extent its traditions survive in our universities today. In addition to toughness and competence, it generated a form of reverence. 'Our law' said Fortescue, 'is a holy sanction or decree commanding those things that be honest, and forbidding the contrary'.

Common Law

The Serjeants were a guild selected by the Crown, usually on the nomination of the judges. The judges (or the bench) were recruited from the Serjeants. Only professional lawyers could be chosen. It was a state, said Fortescue, 'no less worshipful and solemn than the degree of Doctors' (who practised the 'civil law' in cases like those in Admiralty). They were careful then about who could be appointed Serjeants. They had to have been learning and practising the law – they probably saw no difference either way – for at least sixteen years. They took rank above esquires and had equality with knights. (When knighthood was burdensome, the serjeants were exempted.) They had to take an oath of office as follows:

> You shall swear well and truly to serve the King's people as one of the Serjeants-at-law, and you shall truly counsel them that you be retained with after your cunning; and you shall not defer or delay their causes willingly, for covetess of money or other thing that may turn you to profit; and you shall give due attendance accordingly.

Only the word 'cunning' would give us pause now, and we may find it difficult to say why.

The ceremony for new Serjeants might remind you of the Masonic parts in *The Magic Flute*. They were rung out of their Inn by the chapel bell. Wines and cakes were sent to the Inn of the Serjeants. There were elaborate rituals at Westminster – involving multiple *conges* – and the new Serjeant knelt at the feet of the Lord Chief Justice who then put on the coif and the hood and took the oath. There was then a coronation style feast. The King might attend. The festivities might last for seven days. They were expected to hand out rings. Fortescue said the rings 'stood him in fiftie pounds' (ch. 50).

The ceremony was also religious. Churches then, and much later, were used to transact legal business. The Serjeants were allotted 'parvis' at St Paul's. Each stood by his pillar to give advice to his clients. This would have kept down the overheads of practice, and income tax was many centuries away, but it may have taken years to make up for the cost of the initiation rites. Both the King and other litigants paid the Serjeants by liveries of cloth and robes. If you look at the portrait that has come down of Fortescue, with hands in prayer, eyes hollowed a little, you see a man of set learning, shaken and not stirred by the Wars of the Roses, a survivor.

Let us pause. The direction of Edward I on legal education was given by a writ. (The Latin word for writ, *breve*, indicated simply a formal letter.) It concluded that 'those chosen should follow the court and take part in its business; and no others'. The judicial control of education; education for the bench at the bar before the bench; and a monopoly for those so trained (at least if a charge were to be made) are all there 700 years ago. Had education been left to the universities, a more theoretical, or Roman, system would have been likely to have prevailed.

Just as importantly, the only training for the bench was at the bar. It was not offered at a government facility, as was to be the case throughout most of Europe. The bench was part of the legal profession – the top of it, but part of it. Although it was prone to shocking corruption in the form of at least patronage, it had a political independence undreamed of elsewhere. While in their early life the Inns were patronised almost exclusively by the nobility, the law would become a profession giving access to the highest office to those who came from nowhere. For example, Lincoln and Disraeli are prime examples of men of great character and ability who got to the top after starting in the law from nothing, and people who made great contributions to their nations as their leaders. You can add Ghandi and Mandela.

Professor Plucknett thought it desirable to quote the following words of Maitland in full:

> No, the clergy were not the only learned men in England, the only cultivated men, the only men of ideas. Vigorous intellectual effort was to be found outside the monasteries and universities. These lawyers are worldly men, not men of the sterile cast; they marry and found families, some of which become as noble as any in the land; but they are in their own way learned, cultivated

men, linguists, logicians, tenacious disputants, true lovers of the nice case and the moot-point. They are gregarious, clubbable men, grouping themselves in hospices which become schools of law, multiplying manuscripts, arguing, learning and teaching, the great mediators between life and logic, of reasoning, a reasonable element in the English nation.

The Serjeants early had a combative standing that may call to mind the sumo wrestlers of Japan, or the matadors in the Spain of yesterday, or perhaps serious men playing chess in a public place with life-size pieces. But we should recall that their early exchanges were not the kind of oral argument or jury address that we see in court today. Rather, they were the formal statements of position in response to such statements that we call pleadings and which would later come to be put in writing. Tricks were tried, but after all, the bench consisted of men who had gone through the bar.

When we go to the Year Books, we will see that the process is adversarial, but practical and to the point, even if the point was procedural. The bench was not as anxious as many judges are nowadays to make new law. Judges now seem to see that process as necessarily good. Judges then knew that it was necessarily dangerous. They could use the kind of tricks that appellate courts resort to now to avoid confronting unduly sensitive issues (as we will see Mansfield did on the issue of slavery). These cases could be adjourned to allow the parties to settle rather than, as Professor Plucknett said, 'allow the court to be enticed out of its depth'. Professor Plucknett went on:

> The proceedings were therefore as practical as contemporaries could make them; no unnecessary pedantry or cleverness, and above all no oratory. Nowhere during the Middle Ages do we find a trace of rhetoric in the English courts. True to their administrative origin, they kept themselves in a strictly business attitude. It is only after the Renaissance that we find the bad old classical tradition of Greece and Rome which turned law suits into an oratorical contest appearing in England.

A Profession for Lawyers

Note the 'bad old classical tradition' and 'oratorical contest'.

The result was that the two parts, the bench and the bar, worked together. Hostility might look good to some at either end, but it is bad for the delivery of a fair trial. If the two parts work together so well in court, they might even work together against their government. It is hard to see that process at work anywhere else in the world – even now.

The Inns came to play an integral part in the city of London. Shakespeare had the War of the Roses start with the picking of flowers in the garden of the Temple. The first performance of *Twelfth Night* was put on there. You can still get some idea of the tranquillity that may have been on offer if you go through the gardens of Lincoln's Inn, take sustenance in the hall of Gray's, or walk down through the garden of the Temple between the Strand and the Thames. It is a measure of the closeness of the bar and bench that the Serjeants and judges lived together during term time. This was a tradition that of necessity continued for lawyers on circuit. For example, Abraham Lincoln, a very tall man, frequently shared a bed, head to toe, dressed, with his opponent when they travelled on circuit. These facts of life must have offered inducements to settlement.

What became of all this toing and froing in court? The English may subscribe to the view that their laws are not written, but they were prone to write down a lot of what went on. In the Middle Ages, there was no binding doctrine of precedent, but judges and litigants and counsel felt the primal pull of the rule of fairness that like cases should be treated alike. If you want to apply this doctrine properly, you want to write down the cases. You report the cases just as a newspaper reports the news. You need law reports.

The first of these was a series of documents that ran for nearly two hundred years. They were called the *Year Books*. They were written by hand in law French and Latin. The most available edition now was printed hundreds of years later, in Tudor times, in Gothic print, and is now called 'the Standard' or 'Vulgate' edition. They and other reports and sources of law were considered by Professor Percy Winfield in his book, *The Chief Sources of Legal History*. Winfield was called to the bar from the Inner Temple but was in substance an academic. His book was based on lectures given at Harvard.

As Winfield remarked, the Year Books take us into court and keep us there. They are not involved in elementary instruction, and have almost no theory. They resemble notes taken in court and may have been circulated in pamphlet form to update manuals, much as law publishers used to do until recently, before computers took over. They are in many ways like a chatty, down-market form guide. Before investing in a horse, or an argument, you want to see how it has gone over a similar distance and in similar company. A modern title would not be 'advocacy for dummies', but 'handy hints for pleading for lawyers based on real cases'.

Winfield gives us the timely reminder that while we may think that formalism – the preoccupation with law forms – was a disease of the old law, it was in truth its life blood. You tend to find equality, or something like it, between judges and counsel.

> At times it looks as if they and the Serjeants formed a debating society in which the President and officers have, at any rate until the moment for the last word comes, only a nominal precedence, which in no wise prevents them from contributing to the discussion, or from taking vigorous sides in it, and giving and receiving hard dialectical knocks as a consequence.

Rather than looking further into the history of the Year Books, let us take some time to look at some samples from these note books of the apprentices of the law that are the El Dorado of the legal scholar. We can then see how lawyers who ignore the richness of their history deprive themselves, not just of wine, but also of oxygen.

The Countess of Albermale was served with a writ requiring her to answer questions put to her by her King. The lady, by her counsel, prayed judgment on the writ on the contention that it was not specific enough as to what she was required to answer. There was argument before the court. One judge then said,

The law wills that no one be taken by surprise in the King's court. But, if you had your way, this lady would answer in court for what she has not been warned to answer by writ. Therefore she shall be warned by writ of the articles of which she is to answer and this is the law of the land.

Then arose the King, who was very wise, and said: 'I have nothing to do with your disputations, but God's blood! You shall give me a good writ before you arise hence.' In contemporary terms, the accused sought further and better particulars of the pleading and the presiding judge, the King, spat the dummy.

There is a trial before a judge and jury.

> JUDGE: How do you say that he was the next heir?
> THE ASSIZE [JURY]: For the reason that he was son and begotten of the same father …
> JUDGE: You shall tell us in another way how he was next heir, or you shall remain shut up without eating or drinking until tomorrow morning.

One litigant said to the judge, 'Blessed is the womb that bore thee.' Another exchange between counsel and the court:

> COUNSEL: 'Sir, we do not think that this deed ought to bind us, in as much as it was executed out of England.'
> HOWARD J: 'Answer to the deed.'
> COUNSEL: 'We are not bound to do so for the reason aforesaid.'
> HENGHAM CJ: 'You must answer to the deed; and if you deny it, then it is for the court to see if it can try it.'
> COUNSEL: 'Not so did we learn pleading.'

'That is not law now', said one judge in response to another.' 'One more learned than you have adjudged it', retorted counsel.

'The clergy of the province of Canterbury' argued counsel, 'do not meddle with the province of York, and neither is bound by a grant made by the other – "because the Jews have no dealings with the Samaritans".'

One litigant was sent away 'because all the Serjeants agree that the writ could not be supported in this case.' Occasionally the court got firm. 'We forbid you on pain of suspension to speak no further of that averment.' 'That is a sophistry, and this is a place designed for truth.' 'Get you to your business. You plead about one point, they about another, so that neither of you strikes the other.' 'I am amazed that Greene makes himself out to know everything in the world – and he is only a young man.' 'It will go to the winds as does the greater part of that which you say.' 'Not so', said the Chancellor, 'he will have a remedy here in Chancery, for God protects the simple.'

'My client is a poor man and knows no law', argued counsel. 'It is because he knows no law that he has retained you,' was the terse reply of the judge.

Hervey le Stanton gets nicknamed 'Hervey the hasty' and Stanton J conveyed to one attorney the best procedure for him to follow, with a wink.

* * *

If nothing else, lawyers – even judges – are human beings, and the law is the wholly fallible product of their humanity. It is for that reason that a sense of humour is required for the sanity of a lawyer, although judges are not encouraged to lay it on in front of the litigants. The check and counter-check and the word play may be foreign to us, as they are in the early comedies of Shakespeare, but some things remain the same. We can have too much of words or ideas. Winfield was moved to quote the words of Sam Weller (*The Pickwick Papers*) on one voluble magistrate:

> There comes a pouring out, knocking each other's head so fast, that they seems to stun one another; you hardly know what he's arter, do you?

A Profession for Lawyers

But, as ever, we must not get starry-eyed. Some poor bunnies were paying for these lawyers to enjoy their little frolics. It is statistically incontrovertible that nearly one out of every two litigants must lose, and the lawyers frequently arrange affairs so that both sides lose, leaving the lawyers as the only winners. Common lawyers are very good at forgetting the victims. We must never forget that the common law was built on the bones of the broke, the mad, and the dead. Theodore Plucknett said:

> It is impossible to miss the note of admiration for the heroes of the bench and bar which runs through the reports, and the almost excited interest which follows the success or failure of some clever attempt by counsel to maintain a difficult position when called upon to do so. For the contemporary readers who were perfectly familiar with rules of the games, these early Year Books must have read something like vivid newspaper reports of a highly intellectual sport, where even irrelevancies – the quip, the jest, the neat quotation – all have a natural part. Legal science no doubt was their ultimate aim, but they are so full of the joy of forensic battle that one is inclined to look upon them as allied to literature rather than to the cold, impersonal law report of the present day. Throughout the Year Books of Edward II there breathes a spirit of keenness, of combativeness and restlessness which makes them the gayest of law books.

We have to draw the line here, because this is enough to chill the blood. More chilling than that remark about the Battle of Waterloo being won on the playing fields of Eton. No sane person wants to go to court. No sane litigant wants to watch games played in court. Decent judges know that most people look on them as not much better than coppers – someone in authority who may, if given the chance, do them some kind of harm. People just want to get out of court as quickly as they can and with as little damage as possible. Above all, no sane litigant looks to the 'joy' of battle, and we lawyers arrange it so that none of them come out 'gay' at the other end.

Lawyers should always remember the immortal line given to the late Paul Newman in *Butch Cassidy and the Sundance Kid*:

> Butch: What happened to the old bank? It was beautiful.
> Guard: People kept robbing it.
> Butch: It's a small price to pay for beauty.

The need for law reports is not new. Some have said that Moses was the first law reporter. It does appear that the story of the five daughters of Zelophehad in the Book of Numbers was incorporated by Coke in the report of one case and was also cited as a binding precedent by the Jews of Aden who wished to be excluded from the *Indian Succession Act*. But after the Year Books, the law reports become more prosaic.

Later, jurists like Coke got involved in reporting. His reports constituted entire re-arguments to conform with his scheme, a process that has come back into fashion in various parts of the world when scholars go to the bench. Coke was credited with saying that in ancient times the serjeants and apprentices scarcely cited any book or authority by name. He contrasted that practice favourably with the long arguments in his own time in which, he said, 'the farrago of authorities is so great that there must be a good deal of refuse in them'. Heaven only knows how Coke would have responded to written briefs submitted to superior courts in various parts of the world today.

We have reached the modern problem of law reporting. We have far, far too much of it. We have far too much of mediocre judges like toastmasters or best men at weddings wanting their time in the sun – to the annoyance and detriment of the rest of the company. Law reporting has become incessant and unstoppable. We are verging on the point that Gibbon ascribed to Rome of collapsing under the stupendous weight of its own fabric and its own immoderate greatness. It may safely be postulated that if we could get back to the volume and output of the Year Books – ten volumes for say 200 years – the quality of our lives and our litigation would be immeasurably improved.

A Profession for Lawyers

Over time, legal education shifted from the Inns to the universities, although the judges still had the last say. Starting at the bar at the time of the Stuarts was much as it is today. You sought to become known, and might take odd jobs to carry you over. There was initially a probation period – no appearing in court – for ten years. This was reduced to three, and then just ignored. Young barristers could not afford to despise 'pettifogging' attorneys. They may even have schmoozed them. Common Pleas were the preserve of the serjeants. Exchequer was a tax tribunal and therefore both inscrutable and obscure. You might therefore get a brief to do a motion in King's Bench or a junior brief in Chancery. You might perhaps get the odd job at the 'side bar' while the judge robed.

The bar sought to elevate itself by not suing for fees. Barristers were not mere wage earners. They were honorary. The behaviour of some was, as always, appalling. Shortly before the Glorious Revolution, John Evelyn reported:

> I din'ed at my Lord Chancellor's, where being three other Serjeants at law, after dinner being cherefull & free, they told their severall stories, how long they had detained their clients in tedious processes by their tricks, as if so many highway thieves should have met & discovered the severall purses they had taken. This they made but a jest of: but God is not mocked.

Judges were accused of taking bribes and of favouring attorneys. One common complaint against the bar had a distinctly modern ring, and that was that 'to show the Brightness of their Parts, few of them even vouchsafe to look upon their briefs, till the Cause is call'd: and some of them look upon it as an Affront, to be ask'd to peruse 'em before'. *The London Tradesman* warned young barristers against poor barristers being tempted to 'prostitute his Profession by dirty Jobs or demean his Character by espousing causes in themselves villainous'.

But if the young barrister made it, he could make a lot of money. They were not frightened to charge. The case of the Seven Bishops was a *cause célèbre* leading to the Glorious Revolution, but it cost someone a fortune in barristers' fees.

The action on the case was adapted to help commercial men resolve their disputes in the courts. Lord Mansfield brought the bar into business by developing the commercial law and making London a world centre for the resolution of commercial disputes. Industrialisation and the concentration of capital changed the focus of litigation completely. There would be plenty more South Sea bubbles to come. Moreover, to go from Walpole to Gladstone is to change worlds of political morality, and in the Age of Reform the lawyers had to clean up their act generally.

The conclusion of Dr Lemmings is that the 'Inns faded because the logic of the market (economic & political) insisted that the dynamic elements of the English bar should be separate from its ancient institutions, and the profession's centre of gravity shifted accordingly'.

In the thirteenth century it was the barons and their knights who took on the Crown and secured the Great Charter. In the seventeenth century it was the landowners and their lawyers who took on the crown and secured the Bill of Rights. The age of patronage would give way to the industrial revolution and the growth of parties backed by capital and labour. In our own time we have principle-less populists bent on dismantling the Westminster system by responding to opinion polls and the successors to the gutter press.

For many reasons, barristers have been and will be looked on with suspicion. But they are like money-lenders. It takes two to get a deal, bad or otherwise. The Elizabethans liked an old proverb: 'Fools and obstinate men make lawyers rich.' That is still the case, and it is a source of continuing wonderment that the fools and obstinate find each other at either end.

There is something to notice in the rise of the barristers. Professor Richard Pares said we could look at patronage as supplying to people what they can now get from the practice of a profession. He quoted the well-known advice given to young MPs.

A Profession for Lawyers

> Get into Parliament, make tiresome speeches; do not accept them at first, – then do: then make great provision for yourself and family, and then call yourself an independent country gentleman.

Pares later remarks:

> ... the enormous growth of the organized professions – perhaps the greatest change in the whole of modern history – explains, better than anything else, the difference between our attitude to patronage and that of the eighteenth century. We expect to provide for our children by educating them for professions, which can be entered without regard or official favour even when the state is the employer ...

We have seen again in this chapter the emphasis on experience rather than doctrine, on practice rather than theory. A profession that developed like this was not likely to succumb to Roman law, but could have been made for no other purpose than to cause strife with the Crown. To this we must come, but before doing so we must see how these lawyers developed the main parts of the common law dealing with rights between people. We might leave the bar and bench with the tombstone of a lawyer from Norfolk in the time of James I:

> He did profess the law, yet he embraced peace
> Abhorred bribes and therefore now his soul doth live at ease.

VII
Crime, Contract and Negligence

The history of what the law has been is necessary to the knowledge of what the law is.
> Holmes

Order A that justly and truly without delay he perform for B the covenant … and if not … show why he has not done so.
> Medieval Writ of Covenant

Litigation is either civil ('common pleas') or criminal ('pleas of the Crown'). Civil litigation now consists mainly of claims by people that they have been hurt because someone else has been careless or has not kept their word – claims in negligence or for breach of contract. Most of the criminal law is common law. We shall therefore look briefly at the history of crime, contract and negligence. Property, divorce and corporations are mainly dealt with by statute. Actions for trespass are now rare, and usually show bad blood between neighbours, or a dispute about title to land.

Crime

When people praise British justice, they commonly refer to the British criminal law, and procedures taken under it. They may therefore be surprised that a leading historian of English law says this:

Crime, Contract and Negligence

> The miserable history of crime in England can be shortly told. Nothing worthwhile was created. There are only administrative achievements to trace. So far as justice was done throughout the centuries, it was done by jurors and in spite of savage laws. The lawyers contributed humane but shabby expedients, which did not develop into new approaches.

Well, we can understand that reflection on a lack of elegance or precision in the criminal law, but it is nothing to the reflections of those subjected to a casual but unwarranted gaoling in Russia or execution in China.

We saw that under the old German law you could pay for an act of homicide by money. You could buy back the peace that you had broken. A major step in the creation of the criminal law is therefore to make the peace that has been broken the peace of the King, and to have the King, rather than the victim or their family, concerned in protecting their peace and enforcing their law.

You get an idea of how wide was the medieval notion of wrong if you reflect on that for which people ask forgiveness in various versions of the Lord's Prayer – our *debts*, our *trespasses*, and our *transgressions*. The primary writ to vindicate wrongs to the person was the writ of trespass. The Latin for trespass was *transgressio*, and it is illuminating for us that seven hundred years ago people could issue a writ complaining of a 'transgression'. We now issue writs complaining of a wrong (or tort), but the facts that we allege in the complaint have to come within a defined heading of our law of wrongs. As Maitland remarked, trespass, or transgression, was one of the most general terms that you could find, and would 'cover almost all wrongful acts and defaults'.

Glanvill, the first legal text, said that pleas were either civil or criminal. Civil pleas related to land, or what were called personal actions, the antecedents to contract cases that we will look at next. All wrongs, or trespasses, were criminal as they involved an offence against the community as well as the victim. Wrongs that involved violence were dealt with by the writ of trespass. The essence of this action was direct forcible injury. In order to get before the court of the King, the writ had to allege a trespass with violence – 'by force and arms'.

In the way of things, that allegation may have come to be a fiction, and then dispensed with, but an allegation of a breach of the King's peace made the case a plea of the Crown. Under the Great Charter (clause 24) the case was then outside the competence of a lesser court.

Once it is the peace of the government – the King – that is protected, and in the King's court, it would follow that proceedings on behalf of the party aggrieved would be replaced by a communal accusation. The charge would be brought in the name of the Crown – it would be a plea of the Crown – and would be in a form that we describe now as a presentment or indictment. Ominously, the criminal jurisdiction of the royal court was seen as a source of revenue in addition to the revenue the Crown derived from litigation on the civil side.

At about the time of the Great Charter, the church decided that it would no longer take part in the ordeal. The church said this was superstition. A mode of trial that had been used for ages was gone. This change helped to bring in trial by the country – trial by jury. And, to its shame, the law promoted this course by requiring those who did not agree to this mode of trial to submit to torture (called, euphemistically, 'a prison strong and hard'). (We looked at the introduction of the jury in Ch. 3)

Crimes were divided into classes by the common law. The most serious were the felonies. These were the crimes that could not be bought off by compensation. They were 'bootless' crimes. They included murder, which became homicide with malice aforethought; suicide; wounding; rape; arson; burglary; robbery; and larceny. Treason was in a class of its own. Before the word misdemeanour came into use, all crimes less than felonies were simply transgressions (or trespasses).

Barbarous punishments stayed on the books. Bracton said that rape that involved deflowering could attract blinding or castration, and looked back to a time when every rape was a capital offence Most jurisdictions have now codified the laws of theft, but have left the rest of the criminal law in an amended common law form.

Crime, Contract and Negligence

By the time of Coke, the common law required, for the most part, proof of a guilty mind before the Crown could obtain a conviction for the commission of an offence against the criminal law. We saw that Anglo-Saxon law stipulated that people acted at their peril, but the common law came to the more enlightened view. The law stated in the *Institutes* of Coke, gives the *Sermones* of St Augustine as authority (even though the Saint was only talking about perjury).

The aggregation of the law degenerated into as bad and cruel a mess as the law of equity. There were barbarous hangovers that had to await the cleansing scalpel of the Age of Reform of the 19th century. For example, the prisoners, as the accused persons were called, could not give evidence for themselves, compel evidence for their case, or have counsel appear for them.

When speaking of a jury we have not been talking of the form of the jury known as the Grand Jury (or presenting jury). That was a form of inquiry or inquisition into whether there are grounds for charging a person – whether the jury 'should return an indictment' or 'a true bill' – which now only functions in the United States, and elsewhere operates as a reminder of the problems with a closed inquisitorial process.

The law has moved from its preoccupation with revenge. You can compare the slight hesitation of Orestes before he avenges the murder of his father with the agonised hesitation of Hamlet before he avenges the murder of his father. The Sermon on the Mount had altered perspectives over the course of the intervening two thousand years.

The criminal law was the first part of the common law to be methodically expounded. Hale did it in the 17th century, and Hawkins in the 18th. You can still hear *The Pleas of the Crown* of either cited as works of authority. Hale combined a successful career at the bar and bench with a love of scholarship. He also wrote a *History of the Common Law*, and Holdsworth thought that he was a better lawyer than Coke.

The position at the time of Queen Victoria was stated by Sir James FitzJames Stephen as follows:

> A man may disbelieve in God, heaven and hell, he may care little for mankind or society or for the nation to which he belongs – let him at least be plainly told what are the acts that will stamp him with infamy, hold him up to public execration and bring him to the gallows, the gaol or the lash.

Civilized criminal codes have given up the gallows and the lash, but how else have we moved forward?

Contract

Unlike Roman law, German law had no notion of a promise, or agreement, as a source of obligation. It took a long time for the idea of a law of contract to germinate in our common law. This may seem strange if the progression that we are endeavouring to depict is one from status to contract, but it depends on what you mean by contract. Maine also observed that the earliest feudal societies were tied by contract, since the relation of lord to underlings was first settled by express engagement. We have seen the same with the Grand Charter. Maitland was moved to say that 'the idea that men can fix their rights and duties by agreement is in its early days an unruly, anarchical idea. If there is to be any law at all, contract must be taught to know its place'.

We can put to one side the pledge of faith. (This was rather like an undertaking given to a court. The consequences of dishonour were just as radical – in one version, the person making the promise pledged their prospects of salvation.)

We will look briefly at what were called 'personal actions' – as opposed to 'real actions' – before coming to the modern law of contracts. Glanvill said: 'It is not the custom of the court of the Lord King to protect private agreements'

The first writ was a simple action for debt. It was like a claim for restitution of property. The writ directs the court officer – the Sheriff – to require the person said to owe the money to pay what is owing or to attend court to answer the claim. If the Crown was greedy, and *Magna Carta* notwithstanding, this could be a costly exercise. The creditor might have to allow up to one third of recovery to the Crown in fees. But, unlike later, the creditor could claim damages for unlawful detention. One London court allowed 'damages' at 20 per cent. Some jurisdictions still talk of damages by way of interest.

You could get a writ for covenant. This was an action on a sealed document that we would now call a deed. The writ required the defendant 'justly and without delay' to perform the covenant or appear 'to show why he has not done so'. The writ to us looks like it is in the terms of what we now call an order for specific performance. It did not apply to a promise to pay a fixed sum. Thirdly, you could get a writ calling on the other side to give an account of their dealings with you.

You will understand just how remedy-based English common law was if you reflect that these writs were sometimes invoked to procure a judgment as part of the contracting process itself. These writs were sometimes part of the creation of the contract, not its funeral.

But what we call now an action for breach of contract started off in the unlikely place of the writ of trespass. We have seen that a complaint of 'transgression' could embrace a range of wrongs. Why not the wrong of breaking a promise? Well, we are speaking of a time when forms mattered. You had to come within an existing form (of writ or action), and a trespass writ required an allegation of a violent breach of the peace. That is hardly appropriate to a claim that someone has not kept their word.

We will briefly notice the main stages of development.

First, the issuing office, the Chancery, broke down formalism by allowing writs to be issued 'in like case' to existing writs. This licence to reason by analogy used to be attributed to an Act of parliament, the *Statute of Westminster*, but whether or not that is so, the process was hardly novel. Our whole justice system is based on the principle that like cases should be treated alike. This is not confined to us. If you have two dogs, and give a bone to one of them only, your unfairness will be made known to you. Actions started under this facility were called 'actions on the case'.

You can see the growth in five of these 'case' actions in less than ten years in the 14th century. In *The Miller's Case,* the plaintiff said that the defendant had taken his corn at the mill to levy a toll on it. His counsel said. 'I shall have against him such a writ as shall make mention of the circumstances', but the Court ruled that this was a simple trespass. In *The Innkeeper's Case,* a pilgrim at Canterbury sued for loss of goods alleging that it was the use and custom in all England for the innkeeper to keep the goods of guests. This action was held to be good. In *Waldon v Marshall,* the plaintiff claimed that the defendant treated the horse so negligently that it died. This was held to be good because the horse was not killed by force. In *The Farrier's Case,* the farrier lamed the horse, and the court said there was no need to allege 'force of arms' when the action was on the case. This was followed in *The Surgeon's Case.*

Then the courts came to recognise actions for breach of warranty on the footing that the transgression was a form of deception. The person issuing the writ would claim that the defendant knew that the warranty was false, and was therefore fraudulent. In *Doige's Case*, the plaintiff said that he had paid money to the defendant for her promise to convey land to him, but that she had fraudulently conveyed the land to someone else. The plaintiff succeeded, but if the defendant had not 'fraudulently' conveyed the land to someone else, the plaintiff may well have been left to his chances in Chancery. Because of the allegation of deceit, the remedy of restitution appeared to the judges to be appropriate.

Lawyers began to allege that the defendant was indebted to the plaintiff for goods previously sold to the plaintiff. They alleged a debt, and a promise to pay the debt. The great *Slade's Case* did not involve this form of pleading but it is fundamental to the growth of this part of the law. The plaintiff alleged the sale of a crop for £16. There was a finding of a sale, but no other express promise to repay the money. The matter was considered by all the judges 'for the honour of the law'. The court gave judgment for the plaintiff. It ruled that a separate promise (or *asssumpsit*) was to be implied from the transaction raising the debt. Until this decision, a plaintiff suing to recover a debt had had to allege not just the debt, but an undertaking to pay ('being indebted, he undertook to pay'). But this was no longer necessary, since the undertaking was implied from the obligation by the law. Plaintiffs would from then allege express undertakings by the parties, or those implied by law, and these latter provided simple claims for payment for services or goods sold, or work done where no price was fixed.

And so the action in contract broke away from its formal origins. Such a claim must still be founded on a deed, or some benefit to the defendant or detriment to the plaintiff, that the law calls consideration. This was crisply defined in the 16th century in these terms:

> A consideration is a cause or meritorious occasion requiring a
> mutual recompense in fact or law. (*Calthorpe's Case*).

Lord Mansfield tried to assimilate consideration as an element of evidence but his efforts were not sustained.

If the action for breach of contract looks to be a bastard child of odd parents, the same may be said of the doctrine that may yet dispense with the need for consideration. By a process that comes to us from the laws of equity and evidence, a party to an agreement may be precluded from going back on their word if that course seems unconscionable to the court. These cases are raised now in support of claims that could not previously have been made good under the law of contract. This rubric of law is referred to as equitable estoppel.

In the modern law of commerce, the concern is not so much with contract, as with commercial paper, raising capital and allocating risk, and regulating the relations between capital and labour.

Before quitting contract, we must look at one very important offspring – the law of restitution, or unjust enrichment. *Slade's Case* paved the way, but the genius of Mansfield gave it birth. In *Moses v Macferlan,* Moses indorsed four promissory notes in favour of Macferlan. At 30 shillings each the total debt was six pounds. Part of the deal was a written agreement that Moses would have no liability. The notes were not met. Macferlan sued Moses in a local court. That court could not recognize the side deal and Macferlan recovered. Moses then sued for 'moneys had and received to his use'. Macferlan said Moses could only sue on the written agreement. The jury found for Moses after a trial at Guildhall. The point of law was argued (on a Saturday) and Mansfield for the Court ruled in favour of Moses. The defendant was 'under an obligation, from the ties of natural justice, to refund' and 'the law implies a debt and gives this action, founded in the equity of the plaintiff's case, as it were upon a contract …' The obligation to repay is founded in equity – and is invoked to remedy an injustice in a court of common law. It is one of our law's great ironies that the Court where Macferlan won, and the judgment of which was subjected to the equity of the Court of King's Bench, was called he Court of Conscience.

Negligence

We can deal more shortly with the wrong of negligence. It comes to us from three sources.

First, the law has for many centuries – at least six – recognised what we would now call cases of professional negligence in respect of people whose calling is vital to the community, such as carriers, innkeepers and ship masters. A variety of callings were said to be common, since those following them made their services available to everyone – like attorneys or prostitutes. We saw instances of these above – innkeepers, farriers, and surgeons.

The famous case of *Coggs v Bernard* went beyond common callings. What if I without more agree to move your car and it is damaged because I am careless? Bernard agreed to shift several hogsheads of brandy between cellars (in Water Lane) but one cask was staved and many gallons of brandy were lost. Coggs sued for negligence. The jury found against Bernard on the issue of negligence. Bernard objected that no consideration was alleged for the undertaking. The court disallowed the objection, ruling that the undertaking to move the brandy signifies 'an actual entry upon the thing, and taking the trust upon himself' and that the owner's trusting of the defendant with the goods 'is a sufficient consideration to oblige him to a careful management'. This case shows how useful is the notion of 'undertaking'. It conveys an idea of solemnity; it also involves a level of assurance, sometimes even to the point of being a kind of insurance.

A second stream for the modern wrong of negligence came from accidents between strangers such as running down cases on the highway. This was a claim for trespass in the traditional sense. In the second half of the 20th century, an English court had to remind lawyers – in the case of *Fowler v Lanning* – that a claim simply that the defendant 'shot the plaintiff' disclosed no cause of action. What was required was an allegation that the shooting was intentional or negligent. This did not mean that some form of fault had to be alleged or proved. Rather, it meant that the facts alleged had to come within an established category or rubric of legal wrong. The person injured could not simply say that the other side acted at its peril, as in Anglo Saxon times, and the defendant then could seek to rely on some metaphysically sounding doctrine like 'inevitable accident'.

But in a claim for trespass, the injury had to be 'direct'. This rule was in turn relaxed. In *Scott v Shepherd*, a person was hurt after the defendant had thrown a small bomb into a crowd. It was there tossed around in self-defence from hand to hand. It burst and injured the plaintiff. This was held to be 'direct' injury. It is apparent that in a claim for trespass, the complaint was that the defendant had done what they should not have done; in an action 'on the case', the claim was that the defendant had not done what they should have done.

The third stream of authority for negligence involved a relationship between the parties that started in common callings but became wider. These claims were not claims for trespass, but based on an undertaking, or an assumption of responsibility. This is more like our claim in contract.

The final divorce of the wrong of negligence from breach of contract was effected in the US by the decision in *Macpherson v Buick*

Manufacturing Co., and in the UK by the decision in *Donoghue v Stephenson*. In the first case, the plaintiff was injured when the wooden wheel on a Buick car failed. The leading judgment was given by a descendant of Sephardic Jews. Justice Cardozo was later to say of the decision that 'we in the US have been readier to subordinate logic to utility … The development is merely a phase in the assault, now extending along the entire line, upon the ancient citadel of privity'. ('Privity' is the name given to the doctrine that only parties to a contract can sue on the contract).

The second case arose when a lady in Scotland bought what would now be called a ginger beer spider for her friend. When she tipped the ginger beer over the ice cream, the decomposed remnants of a snail came out. Her friend was, not surprisingly, ill. (Or so she alleged in her writ – the decision was given on the pleadings, and the case never went to trial). Since the injured person had not bought the ginger beer, she could only sue for negligence. The leading judgment was given by a Welshman born in Brisbane, Australia. Lord Atkin defined the duty of care by reference to the Sermon on the Mount.

These two precedents are the foundations of the modern law of product liability. They are both avowedly moral and unashamedly legislative, but experience suggests that only judges of the highest calibre – such as these two – can get away with that kind of thing.

One footnote may be permitted to these judgments. That of Cardozo, J is about ten pages in the reports; that of Atkin is about twenty-one pages. Atkin in his judgment refers to the 'illuminating judgment' of Cardozo, and apologises for his own 'long judgment'. Heaven only knows what either of these great judges would have thought of the effusive fulminations of the doom-thunderers of nowadays.

In our time, attention has shifted from adjudicating claims of wrongful hurt between people to distributing loss across the community. People claiming to have been wronged can now bring an action in a class and the alleged wrongdoers frequently have substantial capital behind them. The call for specialised legal representation becomes more insistent, as does the political analysis of the utility of the process.

At the end of his first lecture in *The Common Law*, Holmes said that the criminal law and the law of civil wrongs (or torts) 'started from a moral basis, from the thought that someone was to blame'. Many would put the law of contract on the same footing – although not Holmes, since he took an austere, formal view of the part of the law that we now call the law of contract.

We have seen civil claims split off from criminal actions by a writ that served both, trespass. We then saw an action for non-violent wrongs, the action on the case. From this and other sources came claims for breaches of undertaking, claims in contract. From this claim, and the actions on the case, came our modern claim for negligence. Most of this wrestling with medieval formalism was driven by the need to avoid medieval forms of 'proof.' Parties came to prefer the verdict of a jury. This short history justifies the celebrated comment of Sir Henry Maine that substantive law was secreted in the interstices of procedure.

Does any of this matter to the legal hotshots of the 21st century? It should. The whole of human history teaches us that we cannot work for our future unless we understand our past. The practice of the law is as much a matter of attitude – state of mind – as it is of acquired knowledge or of skill born from experience. And we might remember the remark of Aristotle that 'trying to be more clever than the laws is just what is forbidden by the codes of law that are said to be the best'.

VIII
The Constitutional Settlement

Yet this revolution, of all revolutions the least violent, has been of all revolutions the most beneficent … It is because we had a preserving revolution in the 17th century that we have not had a destroying revolution in the 19th.

Macaulay

The only thing that is missing is what in animals is called 'breeding'. This is a solid inner kernel that cannot be shaken by external pressures and forces, something noble and steely, a reserve of pride, principle and dignity to be drawn on in the hour of trial…. At the moment of truth, when other nations rise spontaneously to the occasion, the Germans collectively and limply collapsed. They yielded and capitulated, and suffered a nervous breakdown….The *Kammergericht* toed the line. No Frederick the Great was needed, not even Hitler had to intervene. All that was required was a few *Amtsgerichtsrats* with a deficient knowledge of the law.

Sebastian Haffner, Defying Hitler

The Stuart kings were roughly handled by the English lawyers. It was not because James I was a dissolute queer, or Charles II an irresolute womaniser; it was not that Charles I and James II affected to be either pious or even Catholic. Rather it was their Christian piety that caused the English to apprehend a threat to their constitution. As we have seen, the first and last articles of the Great Charter guaranteed the freedom of the Church of England. The wording was deliberate. Even back then, there was tension with Rome, but after Luther and Henry VIII, pious dedication by an English king to the Church of Rome was bound to be seen as a threat to the constitution of England – and not just its church. The English Protestants would follow Luther on the need to keep church and state separate, but not on the suggestion that passive obedience to the state was divinely ordained; indeed, the second principle seemed to contradict the first.

In the result, James I and Charles II were suffered to die in their beds (although the latter was prudent enough to undergo a clandestine embrace of the Church of Rome on his death bed). The other two, the pious ones, were not so fortunate. The first was beheaded, and the second was deported, although the English developed the absurd fiction that he had abdicated.

The enduring contribution of the Stuarts to the English constitution is that they settled it – or at least they prompted the English lawyers to do so. The 17th century that saw a civil war and a revolution followed a century that saw a reformation. Here is the context. Osama bin Laden was a serious pest, but he did not launch an Armada to conquer England. *Fatwas* issued by religious fanatics are serial nuisances, but none so far has promised forgiveness, let alone Paradise, for the murderers of the present Queen Elizabeth. We are either bored with or frightened by the excesses of central government now, but no Prime Minister or President is in the habit of offering by virtue of their office dispensations from the laws of their land to their friends or to those who share their faith.

Contrary to a common belief, the English constitution is in writing. It may be said to be contained in two contracts, one writ, and one act of parliament. They are all bound together by the common law; indeed, at this distance, they are all seen as part of the common law. (Two of the compacts were later encased in statute.)

We have looked at the first of these compacts, the Great Charter. It is now time to look at the other three documents, and state the substance of what we understand to be the resulting rule of law.

Given the established preference of the English for a working remedy over a declaration of an abstract right, you will not be surprised to see that the most important of the four documents is a writ. Sir William Holdsworth said that the *Habeas Corpus Act* (31 Charles II, c2) made the writ 'the most effective weapon yet devised for the protection of the liberty of the subject'. (The Act is said by some to have been passed in error. One of the tellers in the Lords was Lord Norris. He was subject to the 'vapours' and suffered a kind of attention deficit syndrome. As a joke, the other teller, Lord Grey, counted one fat lord as ten, but then stuck to it when he saw that Lord Norris had not seen the miscount).

The command of the writ literally says 'you shall have' (*habeas*) 'the body' (*corpus*) but it means that you must produce the person whom you are detaining. Why should we not regard the conduct of depriving someone of their liberty as being unlawful until the contrary is shown to a court of law? The writ is older than *Magna Carta*. Under common law, any free man was entitled if detained other than after criminal conviction or for civil debt to demand from the King's Bench a writ directed to the keeper of the prison commanding him to bring up the body of the prisoner showing the reason for his detention so that the court could judge of its sufficiency. On the return of one of those writs, Lord Mansfield ordered that a negro slave be set free, and effectively outlawed slavery in England.

If you go to any country in the world that is constitutionally off limits – and that means almost any country except those of the common law or in Western Europe – and you have a brush with the law, the one thing you immediately think of is that they probably do not have a mechanism like this to get you out of gaol; and even if they claim to have one, they probably do not have judges who are independent enough to stand up to the current regime. You can have all of the constitutional guarantees, all of the bills of rights in the world, but they are not worth the paper they are written on unless you have an effective remedy for their breach.

You cannot therefore have a government that can say in response to such a writ that the prisoner is held by His Majesty's 'special command'. That would be as bad as the loathsome *lettres de cachet* of Richelieu. Accordingly, one of the parliamentary eruptions against James I, *The Petition of Right*, referred to the 'Great Charter of the liberties of England' and outlawed such a response to this writ. In so doing, the Parliament affirmed the old law that no one could be held 'without being charged with anything to which they might make answer according to the law'. The Petition also outlawed taxes not set 'by common consent in parliament'.

We are getting to the kernel. You cannot be deprived of liberty except by a judgment of a court; you cannot be deprived of property except by a statute of a parliament.

James II was seen to be the worst threat of the lot of the Stuarts. By claiming a dispensing power, he was repudiating the teaching of Bracton that the King was under the law. The English treated his conduct as a repudiation of his contract with them. This entitled them, the argument went, to be discharged from their duties to him, and to be able to enter into a contract with someone who might be better placed to honour such a contract in the future. (This is so under our modern law of contract.) This became *The Bill of Rights*, which became the model for Jefferson's *Declaration of Independence*. It ensured the Protestant succession and dealt with the dispensing power. It then made provision for a standing army, taxation to be levied by parliament, petitions to the Crown, elections, freedom of speech in parliament, excessive bails, trial by jury, and the calling of parliament.

Early in the next century came the *Act of Settlement*, the only essentially statutory part of the English constitution. It ensured the independence of the judiciary by providing that the judges are to be appointed for life – subject to their being of good behaviour. Since then the common lawyers have suspected any judicial officer who does not enjoy that protection and privilege.

So, by the end of the Stuarts, we have securely in place the three elements of the rule of law identified by A.V. Dicey during the reign of Queen Victoria. Before saying what they were, Dicey referred to de Tocqueville. He found England to be 'much more republican' than Switzerland. It was said by de Tocqueville that:

> The Swiss seem to still look upon associations from much the same point of view as the French, that is to say, they consider them as a means of revolution and not as a slow and sure method of obtaining redress of wrong … The Swiss do not show the love of justice which is such a strong characteristic of the English. Their courts have no place in the political arrangements of the country, and exert no influence on public opinion. The love of justice, the peaceful and legal introduction of the judge into the domain of politics, are perhaps the most outstanding characteristic of a free people.

The first element identified by Dicey was the absolute supremacy of regular law over arbitrary power. This was the supremacy of law over people. Aristotle had, after all, said that 'the rule of law is preferable to that of any individual'. This explains the reaction against the Law Lords in the decision in *Shaw v DPP*, with H.L.A. Hart comparing the decision with German statutes of the Nazi period which condemned anyone who was deserving of punishment according to the 'fundamental conception of a penal law and sound popular feeling'.

The second aspect of Dicey was equality before the law, or the equal subjection of all classes to the ordinary laws of the land.

The third part is characteristic of the common law. We see the constitution as the result of the ordinary law of the land. The constitution is not the source, but the consequence, of the rights of individuals. The constitution is itself part of the common law. The Europeans tend to see it the other way around – they see private rights deriving from public institutions. Dicey said, 'Our constitution, in short, is a judge-made constitution, and it bears on its face all the features, good and bad, of judge made law'. He went on to say that, 'the Habeas Corpus acts declare no principle and define no rights, but they are for practical purposes worth a hundred constitutional articles guaranteeing individual liberty'. This is as close to dogma as the common law gets.

With the Revolution came the final burial of an inquisitorial court called the Court of Star Chamber. This was an ancient offshoot of the council of the king, as is the Privy Council, still. The name Star Chamber is a byword for English lawyers or any body of a judicial type set up outside what we call the rule of law. One example is Guantanamo Bay. If as counsel you want to get well and truly off-side with such a bureaucratic inquisition, walk in ostentatiously bearing the treatise of Sir Edward Hudson on *The Court of Star Chamber*.

We pause to notice two consequences of the rule of law as it developed in England. They may seem inevitable to us now, but they were not then in England, let alone anywhere else. By the working of the common law, the English outlawed torture and slavery. Just how remarkable are those achievements is demonstrated by the fact that it took a civil war before the Americans could achieve the second, and they are now seeking to dismantle the first in the name of a war that the rest of the world regards as phoney.

Precious little philosophy was invoked to get these results. John Locke had more influence in the US than in England (and it is certain that Rousseau had more influence in France and Hegel in Germany than Locke had anywhere). This is how the US political scholar W.A. Dunning described the working out of Locke's theories in English law:

> It was a theory of a state of nature that was not altogether bad, and its transformation into a civil state that was not altogether good, by a contract that was not very precise in its terms or clear in its sanction. It embodied, moreover, a conception of sovereignty of the people without too much of either sovereignty or people; of the law of nature that involved no clear definition of either law or nature; of natural rights, but not too many of them; and of a separation of powers that was not too much of a separation. It concluded, finally, with a doctrine as to the right of revolution that

left no guarantee whatever for the permanence of the rather loose-jointed structure which the rest of the theory had built up. Yet this illogical, incoherent system of political philosophy was excellently adapted to the constitutional system which England needed at the time and which the Whigs actually put and kept in operation.

This precisely captures the element of perversity in England constitutional growth.

We are back then with the difference between England and Europe that runs through these pages. Two things may be said. First, the closest that the English have come to a dictator who was a war criminal was Cromwell. He was certainly a dictator and in our eyes he was certainly a war criminal for what he did in Ireland (and in the eyes of the only other person to whom the English have put up a statue outside their Parliament – Winston Churchill; see his expressions of outrage in his *History of the English Speaking Peoples*, 'By an uncompleted process of terror … upon all of us lies "the curse of Cromwell"'). England has not produced anyone who has come even close to Napoleon, Stalin, Hitler, Franco or Mao. The reasons why are referred to in outline here, especially in the remarks of Macaulay and Haffner at the start of this chapter.

The second issue has not been sufficiently noticed. If you ask a German lawyer, or a French lawyer, to give an opinion according to the methods of the common law they will have a problem. The reverse holds true. If you seek to get a common lawyer to answer a question by reference to the methods of a European lawyer, they will have a problem. If you overlay the common law with an absolute law imposed from above, the common lawyer immediately has a problem. The law is foreign. You can see it all the time as the Americans wrestle with the rights or liberties granted from on high, such as the freedom of speech or the right to bear arms.

The Australians got into awful trouble with a provision in their constitution that said trade between the States had to be 'absolutely free'. What from? 'Absolutely'? How absolute is absolutely? Were they not taught that there are no degrees of 'absolute"? The best minds in the country – in the world, some thought – got themselves into metaphysical knots that they had not been trained to undo. Finally, the supreme court of the nation changed its approach, looked at the history of the debates, and gave a short, sensible interpretation that is politically and historically unanswerable, and which killed off a minor but useless cottage industry (*Cole v Whitfield*).

Trying to put anything resembling a code over the common law is like mixing Tuscan olive oil with Devonshire cider or a Moselle riesling with Yorkshire ale. They just do not mix. We need to bear this simple proposition in mind when discussing possible constitutional amendments or a bill of rights over and above the *Bill of Rights* that we already have. It may be harmless enough if the new model is not binding, but not so if it is. We know by now who the only certain winners will be from further interference with our laws. We have long since left the phase of thinking that change to the law *must* be good, and we should be educating ourselves to the fact that changing the laws means adding to them, and is likely on that ground alone to make them worse.

Before leaving the Glorious Revolution, we might notice one Old Whig for whom it was a glorious reality. William Blackstone came from Cheapside. He got a foundation place at Charterhouse and later a fellowship at All Souls. All his life he preferred its society to that of the Middle Temple. He found his companions at the bar to be 'obscure and illiterate'. English law needed a readable treatise. Blackstone delivered, with nine human progeny to boot. The four volumes of his *Commentaries on the Laws of England* grew out of lectures he gave at Oxford. They paved the way for the standard texts on narrower fields that followed in the next century. More importantly, they achieved biblical status in the US as stating and defining their common law inheritance. A failure at the bar and on the bench, his celebration of the constitution and common law gave him a lasting pre-eminence in the New World.

Common Law

We may finally observe that while the common law developed by techniques very different to those of Roman law, the two systems had a lot in common in the way in which they settled their constitutions. The English got theirs from the process and profession of the common law and a distrust of philosophy. Professor Dunning said this:

> The English constitution, like the Roman, was a product of practical political sagacity, administrative ability, and a spirit of legalism in the dominant classes; and the later system owed as little to the scholastic political theories that prevailed on the Continent, as the earlier system owed to the refinements of Greek speculation.

The English were concerned with the rights of Englishmen, not the Rights of Man. It would be left to the poet John Milton to come up with something large and poetical like 'No man, who knows aught, can be so stupid as to deny, that all men naturally were born free …'

For both Rome and England the process took hundreds of years of trial and error. This might be borne in mind by those who think that this model for government can be packed up like a car ready to take off smoothly in the hands of someone who has never seen much less driven one before.

IX
Judges and Jurists

To recall the judges and the jurists of the 19th century may be an antidote to the most vulgar and provincial of modern heresies – the indifference or contempt for any age but our own, the impudent assumption that the world belongs to the living and is a property in which the dead hold no shares.

Fifoot

Raleigh: Mr. Attorney, have you done?
Coke: No, I will have the last word for the King.
Raleigh: No, I will have the last word for my life.
Coke: You are an odious fellow; you are hateful to all the realm of England for your pride.
Raleigh: It will go near to prove a measuring cast between you and me, Mr. Attorney.

Notable Historical Trials

You cannot understand the laws of a country without knowing something of the history of those laws, and you cannot understand that history without knowing something of the history of the country. The best way to approach it is by looking at the lives of those who made it. We will look at notable judges and jurists to tie up the developments that we have been talking of, and to bring us up to our own time.

Sir Edward Coke

Sir Edward Coke (pronounced 'Cook') represents a lot that is good and a lot that is not so good in the common law. The son of a barrister, born in Norfolk, he was, most unusually for a lawyer of those times, educated at a university – Trinity College, Cambridge. He said students should come to the common law from university where they could learn 'the liberal arts and especially logick'. He was called to the bar at the Inner Temple, and soon acquired a large practice. He served as Solicitor-General, Attorney-General, Speaker of the House of Commons, Chief Justice of Common Pleas, and Chief Justice of King's Bench. He was also famous as the author of *The Reports* and *The Institutes*. He died a very wealthy man.

Coke was not frightened to change his mind or his position, which was just as well for someone capable of behaviour that would now be called manic-depressive. He was handsome in appearance (which he was careful to maintain) and, as Holdsworth drily remarked, 'this always went some way with James I'. If you look at the Van Dyke portrait, you can sense why he could have proved a handful for both princes and prisoners – there is about him something of the Burmese cat and something of the ballet principal, of the smaller *danseur noble* variety. He married twice. His second wife, Lady Hatton, had wealth to match his and an ego in the same category. He won her over his great rival, Bacon, but they were greatly unsuited to each other. A neighbour said that 'Lord Coke is tossed up and down like a tennis ball'.

His behaviour toward Raleigh was, by the standards of today, appalling. Sir James Stephen said of his conduct:

> The extreme weakness of the evidence was made up for by the rancorous ferocity of Coke, who reviled and insulted Raleigh in a manner never imitated, so far as I know, before or since in any English court of justice, except perhaps those in which Jeffreys presided.

But if Coke could be rabid in going in to bat *for* the King, he could be just as tough *against* the King. Upon elevation to the bench,

Coke underwent a conversion like that of Becket when he became Archbishop. Their elevations became them. Early in his reign, James I told Coke he thought he could do as well as the judges. Coke reminded the King that he was not a lawyer. The King then got very hot and asked if he was supposed to be under the law. As we know, Bracton had said just that, and Coke said so. After which, 'his Majestie … looking and speaking fiercely with bended fist offering to strike him, which the lord Coke perceiving fell flat on all fower'. As Professor Plucknett said, 'the King lost his dignity and Coke his nerve'. Roscoe Pound, no sentimentalist, would later describe this 'Sunday-morning conference' as 'the glory of our legal history'.

Coke even went as far as to say that the judges could declare an act of parliament to be void if they thought that the act was unreasonable. Regrettably, for some, that doctrine did not gain acceptance. Coke was unremitting in his resistance to the powers of the crown which were summed up under the weasel word 'prerogative'. Ironically, it was Coke's development of writs called 'prerogative writs' that led to the control of the powers of government and to our modern administrative law. These writs are formally issued in the name of, or at the suit of, the Crown, but as a matter of substance they issue on behalf of (*ex parte*) a subject, and they call on a government official to justify their conduct toward that subject before the court. Critics said that the decisions and proclamations of Coke 'import as if the King's Bench had a superintendency over the government itself, and to judge wherein any of them do misgovern'. That looks to be precisely what Coke had in mind.

Strong-willed, and hot-tempered, Coke looks like he was both willing to wound and not afraid to strike. But you have the impression with him that you would carry those wounds down your front.

As well as fighting with his King, Coke fought with equity judges, especially Bacon and Ellesmere. These were what we would now call turf wars. The Court of Star Chamber was of course anathema. Trouble pursued Coke and he pursued it. He was prosecuted before the ecclesiastical courts over an irregularity in his second marriage. He was later to spend seven months in the Tower on a charge of treason, this during a time when such a fate would frighten any sane subject near to death. He passed his seventieth birthday there. But during an interlude in his career, it was he in the House of Commons who presented *The Petition of Right* to the House and secured its passing. He had said that 'Magna Carta is such a fellow that he will have no sovereign'. It now had a partner.

Sir William Holdsworth said that Coke was essentially a Tudor statesman who did not realise that the time of the Tudor statesmen had passed. But Coke had 'cemented the old alliance between parliament and the common law, to which in the past both the common law and parliament owed so much'. It is impossible to over-estimate the importance of this league between the judiciary and the parliament against the Crown. Trevelyan, a great-nephew of Macaulay, got downright lyrical.

> Coke had not striven in vain. He had enlisted the professional pride of the students of the common law against the rival systems especially favoured by the Crown and the Star Chamber, the Admiralty and the Ecclesiastical Court. He had turned the minds of the young gentlemen of the Inns of Court, who watched him from afar with fear and reverence, to contemplate a new idea of the constitutional functions and of political affinities of their profession, which they were destined in their generation to develop in a hundred ways, as counsel for England had gone to the law with her King.

This is a large notion which bears reflecting upon. Maitland referred to 'an incarnate national dogmatism, tenacious of continuous life'. If not the hero of the nation, Coke was certainly the champion of the common law. He had stood, sometimes alone, against two powerful monarchs, who thought they were anointed by God, at a time when politics were fought hand to hand, face to face, and with very ugly and terminal results for the loser. All his life Coke showed immense moral and personal courage. He was shifted, then sacked, then reviled. As tough as old boots, James I paid him the supreme compliment. 'Throw this man where you will, and he falls upon his legs'. If in the 1920's Sebastian Haffner had asked who in England may have embodied that 'solid inner kernel' and 'steely reserve of pride' that he thought his nation had missed, the answer may have been Edward Coke. Carlyle called him 'one of the toughest men ever made'.

Lord Mansfield

Lord Mansfield was born William Murray, the fourth son of an impoverished Scottish peer who took part in the 1715 rising. He became a King's Scholar at Westminster and went on to Christ Church, Oxford. There he won a competition for a Latin poem on the death of George I, beating Pitt in the contest. In reading law he preferred Scottish texts to English. He acquired an aversion to the work of Coke. He was introduced to Pope who had a lasting effect on his thinking and speaking. One of his big early cases was for the defence in *Cibber v Sloper*. Sloper had been found in bed with Cibber's wife, but as the evidence came out it appeared that Sloper had rented more than the room from Cibber. Edward Burke made a most illuminating remark about the real power of a true advocate:

> He had some superiors in force, some equals in persuasion; but in insinuation he was without a rival. He excelled in the statement of a case. This of itself, was worth the argument of any other man.

A few – very few – advocates safely carry this power to the bench. Governments tend not to like such judges.

Mansfield went on to become the Lord Chief Justice of England for thirty-two years. Before that he had entered parliament on the Whig side and had served as both Solicitor-General and Attorney-General. He became deeply unpopular and his house was burnt down during the Gordon Riots. (He later presided over the trial of Gordon: he concluded his charge to the jury at 4.30 of the second morning of the trial.)

He left a lasting impression on almost every aspect of English law. He was, like Lord Denning, personally conservative, but radical on the bench. His views were on some issues radical to the point of being heretical, and had he expressed them on religion a century or so earlier he could have found himself tied to a stake.

He knew how to get through the business. He decided about 700 causes a year. He made a point of clearing his list at least once each term and he often rose at one or two o'clock in the afternoon. He knew that delay is the fault of the lawyers, not the litigants. He outlawed adjournments even by consent. He is said to have originated the English practice of giving judgment on the spot, and our loss of that facility is one of the reasons that we are now going backwards. He understood that business flows into the court of a good judge.

He took especial care to try to make commercial law simple. He said that the law had to be set out in rules easily learnt and easily retained because they are the dictates of common sense. Merchants have no need to speculate or wonder what the law might be. In one case he awarded damages for breach of copyright, as we would now call it, notwithstanding the indignant refusal by Lord Hardwicke to grant an injunction (*Blanchard v Hill*). The case of *Moses v Macferlan* was a great case on the basis of which a huge amount of learning on the law of restitution has developed. The manuscript note of Mansfield of the case takes about a page in contemporary text. The jury returned a verdict for £6, reserving one matter for the opinion of the judges. Costs were fixed in the additional amount of £22. Note that this case, as did almost all involving Mansfield, required a jury. Mansfield used to empanel 'special juries' of people knowledgeable of the commercial customs of London and England in order to help him settle the commercial law.

In a judgment which affirms that 'the Constitution does not allow reasons of state to influence our judgments', he reversed the outlawry of the agitator Wilkes on grounds that had not been taken by counsel for Wilkes. He sought to avoid ruling on slavery because of the dependence of so much trade upon it, but when required to rule, he did not flinch. His judgment in the case of *Somerset* is a model and may be set out in large part:

> We are so well agreed, that we think there is no occasion of having it argued (as I intimated an intention first) before all the judges, as is usual, for obvious reasons, on a return to a Habeas Corpus. The only question before us is, whether the cause on the return is sufficient? ... The state of slavery is of such a nature, that it is incapable of being introduced on any reasons, moral or political, but only by positive law, which preserves its force long after the reasons, occasion, and time itself from whence it was created, is erased from memory. It is so odious, that nothing can be offered to support it, but positive law. Whatever inconvenience, therefore, may follow from this decision, I cannot say this case is allowed or approved by the law of England; and, therefore, the black must be discharged.

It may well be that because Mansfield was broadly educated and not brought up in the minutiae of common law procedure he was able to adopt such an expansive view and mode of working with the law. In the eyes of many, there is only one English judge since who might claim to be in the same class. The sketch of Mansfield held at the Boston Athenaeum reveals what must be the most commanding judicial presence since Moses; this is the very portrait of authority, what the Romans called *auctoritas*.

A nephew of Mansfield took a black woman from a Spanish vessel and brought her to England. She bore him a child. Mansfield maintained her in his family. He named her Dido. A visiting governor of Massachusetts recorded that 'He knows he has been reproached for showing fondness for her – I dare not say criminal'. She would come to write letters for him when he was passed it. In his will, he confirmed her freedom and said that she had 'always honoured (him) with uninterrupted confidence and friendship.'

Lord Eldon

Lord Eldon is a different proposition altogether. He came from a successful family of 'fitters' (coal factors) in Newcastle. Born John Scott, he was educated at the local grammar school. He fell in love with Elizabeth Surtees. All parents objected to the union. Eldon took up a ladder and eloped. This was the one great act of rebellion in his life, and it is almost as if he spent the rest of his life in expiation, although the union appears to have been both enduring and happy.

Like Mansfield, Eldon served in each of the Law Offices. He was a kindly person commendably unhappy when leading politically sensitive prosecutions, and with a commendable capacity to lose them. He was accused of descanting on his humanity. He was for a very short time a judge of common law, but he went on to become Lord Chancellor for about twenty five years. He was, ideologically, the most earnest of Tories. He became a brazen reactionary and unrepentant troglodyte, attributes sadly admired and occasionally mimicked by his adorers, especially those in the colonies. He opposed any kind of reform, such as Catholic Emancipation, the Great Western Railway, the Reform Act, the repeal of the Test Acts, and anything else that might threaten the status quo. It is said that the only reform measure that he ever supported was the abolition of trial by battle. (A man charged with murder thought this was a good wheeze to try to beat conviction.) With no knowledge of or respect or common humanity, Doctor No, as he would be called, opposed any inquiry into the system as it would 'sanction a suspicion' that something may be wrong.

If you look at the main portrait of Eldon you are looking at someone at once both supercilious and predatory, nearly submerged in the suffocating regalia of the highest rank. Eldon remained courteous but he took equity into a morass and was savagely attacked for it by Dickens: 'The one great principle of the English law is to make business for itself.' (*Bleak House*). He suffered from a defect which, after prejudice, is the worst that can affect a judge – he was afraid to decide. It is said that he once expressed doubts upon a will after thinking about it for twenty years – 'there can be no use in taking more time to consider it'. In another case, he sat on his judgment for so long that everyone at the bar table had forgotten the facts. Perhaps his swift escalation into the heights of the conservative establishment from a family of trade near the border ensured that he would be as implacably reactionary as he was. As one biographer remarked, with the habit of mind that he had, 'an adherence to the status quo became less a dogma than an inevitable consequence'. Yet, when he died, he had amassed a fabulous fortune from his holding of his various public offices and the practice of the law. He died in misery. The Age of Reform was at hand, and only God could save 'the men of property, the men of sound religious character, the men of rank, the nobility and the Crown in this disordered country'.

His admirers say he gave equity the same structural solidity as the common law. Was that what it was invented for? Those who celebrate the legal achievements of Eldon are too quick to forget the human misery on which it was built, and the betrayal of the ancient promise that justice would not be delayed, sold, or denied. Nor was he hanging out for stylistic elegance. Holdsworth began his list of the defects of Eldon as follows: 'First, Eldon was nothing but a lawyer … He had no literary skill, no literary taste, no idea of literary style. Hence his judgments, which he never took the trouble to write, are formless things'. Eldon had a real Newcastle burr, but it must have taken real *chutzpah* to reserve judgment for years and then not produce a written text but, as Lord Denning was to put it, give it 'off the reel'.

With Mansfield and Eldon you can see almost a caricature of the difference between common law at its best and equity at its worst. Mansfield was quick while Eldon was slow. Mansfield looked forward while Eldon looked backwards. Mansfield simplified while Eldon extended and complicated the law. Mansfield wanted change but Eldon resisted it, literally to the death. Mansfield wanted the law to grow but Eldon wanted it to stay as it was, except that there would be more of it.

Oliver Wendell Holmes

Oliver Wendell Holmes was born into the American aristocracy, the Boston Brahmins, and it showed. Gareth Jones concluded a short biographical note: 'It is not surprising to learn that he never read a newspaper.' He was for most of his life in the shadow of his father. After a brilliant career he was still, at the age of 61, described as the son of Dr Holmes.

He enlisted as a private soldier in the 20th Massachusetts Regiment, known as the Harvard Regiment. During the war he fought in some of its most vicious battles, and stopped three bullets. Before the war, a friend made a very modern remark: 'I wish Wendell wouldn't play with his mind'. He returned 'a Romantic hero built for it'. That history could incline any man to become philosophical and in the case of Holmes, it inclined him to fatalism, the overt rejection of large principles, and a devotion to paradox.

It also led him to say that experience was much more important than logic in the life of the law, although his philosophical temperament from time to time drove him to conclusions as a matter of logic that to us are unpalatable. It was, however, entirely within character that he should begin his discussion of 'Possession' as follows: 'It will be a service to sound thinking to show that a far more civilized system than the Roman is framed upon a plan which is irreconcilable with the *a priori* doctrines of Kant and Hegel.' He went on to refer to a German writer who 'expresses a characteristic yearning of the German mind when he demands an internal juristic necessity drawn from the nature of possession itself, and therefore rejects empirical reasons'. He was fond of exalting experience over logic, practice over theory, and experiment over dogma. His devotion to the intellect was puritanical, but it was the intellect of practical reason, one that involved a total rejection of the mysteries of metaphysics.

After the war, he qualified for his law degree after three terms (a course which he was later to argue against). He practised in partnership and taught at Harvard. Shortly after he published *The Common Law* he was offered a professorship at Harvard and then a position on the Supreme Court. (Thayer did not forgive him for walking out on Harvard so quickly.) A Justice of the Supreme Court of the United States for thirty years, he is probably the best known American judge and jurist outside his own country.

To read the correspondence between Holmes and Pollock is to enter into a world of almost ascetic learning that we will never recapture, even if we wanted to. But for all his aloofness, Holmes was not unaware of other forces at work in the world. In his 90th year he remarked to Pollock on the tendency of modernist painting to vanity and 'lewd' desire: 'To do something damned smart right off, just as skirt dancing offers, as a substitute for the training that makes a "danseuse", a suggestion that you may see a little more at the next high kick.' It was said that English women remembered Holmes in the 1890s as 'the most perfect flirt in London', a man who had a 'provocative gleam' in his eye. He may only have fallen back on skirt dancers later.

He professed indifference to all legislation to make people better, as a Boston Brahmin well might do, and said that he saw 'no meaning in the rights of man except what the crowd will fight for'. It was probably this kind of attitude that led William James to say of Holmes that he had a 'cold blooded, conscious egotism and conceit'.

But the scholarly analysis of *The Common Law* stands in its own right, and his judgments have at times the lapidary quality of the speeches of Lincoln. Here is well known example:

> Persecution for the expression of opinion seems to me to be perfectly logical. If you have no doubt of your premises or your power and want a certain result with all your heart you naturally express your wishes in law and sweep away all opposition. When men have realised that time has upset many fighting faiths, they may come to believe even more than they believe the very foundation of their own conduct that the ultimate good desired is that reached by free trade in ideas – that the best test of truth is the power of thought to get itself accepted in the competition of the market, and that truth is the only ground upon which their wishes safely can be carried out. That, at any rate, is the theory of

our Constitution. It is an experiment, as all life is an experiment. Every year if not every day we have to wage our salvation upon some prophecy based upon imperfect knowledge. While that experiment is part of our system, I think that we should be eternally vigilant against attempts to check the expression of opinion that we loathe and believe to be fraught with death …
(*Abrams v United States*).

Holmes had the real genius of the best common lawyer: he could see the real issue, and state it simply and shortly. He said he had 'hankered after philosophy'. He fell into the law as if by default. He did not regret it; nor did he not become a philosopher. He is surely the most philosophical judge and jurist that the common law has produced.

Frederic William Maitland

Frederic William Maitland is entitled to be remembered as the scholar's scholar, if not the historian's historian. He came from a family of service. He went from Eton to Trinity College, Cambridge, where he gained a running blue. He was smart enough to be elected to the 'Apostles' and smart enough not to let it ruin him – it was a self-important group of intellectuals that does not seem to have done anything for the humility or sexual stability of most of its members. He married Florence Fisher, a niece of Leslie Stephen. He did not succeed greatly at the bar, but he discovered early that his interest was in history.

Maitland was to become one of the creators of English history, and the father of English legal history. He brought order out of chaos and knew that to understand the laws of a community is to understand its ideas and motives. He constantly warned of looking at the past through the eyes of today. He produced the monumental *History of English* Law with Pollock. Although Pollock contributed very little, Maitland put his name on the title page, and with first billing.

His attachment to history did not preclude him from trying to rid the law of anachronism: 'accidents will happen in the best regulated museums'. But he told Pollock 'I have no use for modern kings'. He saw keenly the difference between the lawyer and the historian.

'What the lawyer wants is authority and the newer the better; what the historian wants is evidence and the older the better.' He thought Maine was too prone to make large statements detached from detailed evidence.

His affection for the Germans could have got the better of him. He named his children Ermengard and Fredegond and he liked Wagner. But Florence was strong too. They had had a Victorian courtship – it was an occasion to celebrate when they were 'allowed to go about without a keeper'. Florence did not relate to the wives of other dons, and she did not relish visits from Pollock. She was a refined pianist – she played for Tchaikovsky before pinning a flower on his lapel when he was awarded an honorary doctorate.

Maitland suffered bad health all his life. He said he was buffeted by 'the messenger of Satan'. He was an appalling subject for photographers, and looks like a haunted version of Wittgenstein. He had to winter every year in the Canaries and died there early last century after he caught pneumonia. He comes down to us now as a kind of saint, a modest scholar who cast light on our past. It is a measure of his greatness that when we read Macaulay now, we ask – where is the law? Maitland was one of those Englishmen in whom history and literature are fused in life. He was, surely, as true and loyal a chronicler and celebrant as his nation has produced.

Benjamin Cardozo

Benjamin Cardozo spent nearly twenty years as a judge in New York before spending six years on the US Supreme Court, taking the seat of Oliver Wendell Holmes.

His ancestors were Sephardic Jews. His father was tied up in the Tammany Hall scandals, but Cardozo went on to graduate from Columbia College before practising at the New York bar. He never married, and had to put up with the nonsense that that condition provokes.

His writings off the court made him a national figure. For our taste now, they are perhaps a little overwrought, but they were directed to students and continuing members of the profession in an effort to uphold what Cardozo saw as the best in the profession. By contrast, his judgments were shorter and although he was fond of the epigram, he was not a judge of the romantic view of the world. He had a significant effect on revolutionising the law of wrongs, as in the case of *Macpherson v Buick Motors*. As we saw, his judgment in that big case was ten pages long. Some appellate courts now take that long to state the facts even though it has obviously been done before. Here is the paragraph in which Cardozo stated the facts and the issue:

> The defendant is a manufacturer of automobiles. It sold an automobile to a retail dealer. The retail dealer resold to the plaintiff. While the plaintiff was in the car, it suddenly collapsed. He was thrown out and injured. One of the wheels was made of defective wood, and its spokes crumbled into fragments. The wheel was not made by the defendant; it was bought from another manufacturer. There is evidence, however, that its defects could have been discovered by a reasonable inspection, and that an inspection was omitted. There is no claim that the defendant knew of the defect and wilfully concealed it. The case, in other words, is not brought within the rule … The charge is one, not of fraud, but of negligence. The question to be determined is, whether the defendant owed a duty of care and vigilance to anyone but the immediate purchaser.

When we come to the lectures, the tone tends to get ethereal if not romantic.

> Skill is not won by chance. Growth is not the sport of circumstance. Skill comes by training, and training, persistent and unceasing, is transmuted into habit. The reaction is adjusted ever to the action. What goes out of us as effort comes back to us as character. The alchemy never fails.

On the Supreme Court, he dissented from the avoidance of New Deal legislation sponsored by Roosevelt. But the court did not see the best of him. He thought it was 'more politics than law'. He led the charge in destroying the fiction that judges do not make law.

If you look at the portraits of Cardozo you see a curious mixture of granitic strength and aquiline sharpness, but in the end there is no want of benevolence. Goodhart said '…he had an almost feminine charm. He gave one, in an indefinable way, a feeling that here was a man who, without losing his humanity and sympathy, represented in his life the highest ideals that a man can hold…'

Roscoe Pound

Roscoe Pound was born shortly after the end of the American civil war and died in the year that the Olympics were held in Tokyo. He was variously a scholar, generalist, professor, dean, reformer and trial lawyer. He had three degrees, including a Ph.D. in Botany, but no law degree. During his time studying at Harvard, he was taken with the teaching of Professor John Gray.

Around the end of the 19th century, he handled many cases as a trial lawyer before juries in Nebraska cowtowns, and he later served as a Commissioner of Appeals in the Nebraska Supreme Court. Early in the 20th century he wrote an article for the ABA that became influential on 'The Causes of Popular Dissatisfaction with the Administration of Justice'. His experience at the frontier left him with a distaste for the trial as a 'forensic gladiatorial show' and wishing that common law ideals might be relieved 'from the yoke of crudity and coarseness which the frontier sought to impose upon them'. He taught at Harvard and was Dean for 20 years.

The range and quantity of his writings is vast, and it is work of great scholarship informed by experience at the bar. It is very hard to imagine Holmes before a Nebraska jury, but it is easy to imagine him in deep philosophical dialogue with Roscoe Pound. Pound concluded

Common Law

his preface to *The Spirit of the Common Law* with a reference to the interventions challenging it:

> When the lawyer refuses to act intelligently, unintelligent application of the legislative steamroller by the layman is the alternative.

Here is how he said at the end of his book that the common law could answer its challengers:

> For through all vicissitudes the supremacy of law, the insistence upon law as reason to be developed by judicial experience in the decision of causes and the refusal to take the burden of upholding right from the *concrete each* and put it wholly upon the *abstract all* have survived. These ideas are realities in comparison whereof rules and dogmas are ephemeral appearances. They are so much a part of the mental and moral makeup of our race, that much more than legal and political revolutions will be required to uproot them. (Emphasis added)

This book continues to talk to us because it is an elevated view of the reception of the common law into the New World; it is in truth a masterpiece of original analysis and writing, worlds apart from what passes as scholarship elsewhere.

But Pound remembered what it was like to come up the hard way.

> Immunity of accused persons from all interrogation, if they are firm, well-advised and able to give bail, is a most effective shield of wrongdoer ... No rich man has been subjected to the third degree to obtain proof of violation of anti-trust or anti-rebate legislation, and no powerful politician has been so dealt with in order to obtain proof of bribery or graft.

Roscoe Pound is commonly ranked as the most significant scholar of the law produced in the US, and he got there without a law degree. He comes to us now like Holmes, a raw uncut diamond.

Alfred Thompson Denning

Alfred Thompson Denning was known throughout his life as Tom to his friends. He came from the family of a draper in Hampshire. Denning was brought up to avow not only the King James Bible and Shakespeare, but also *A Pilgrim's Progress*. He went to a grammar school and from there on a scholarship to Magdalen at Oxford. He got First Class Honours in Mathematics and Law.

Like Holmes, Denning put on the uniform, and the course of World War I had nearly as much impact on Denning as the Civil War had on Holmes. One of his brothers attained the rank of General in World War II, but another brother died of tuberculosis after the battle of Jutland. Denning never forgave Admiral Jellicoe for not having a go in trying to finish off the German fleet. Denning was never to be in awe of rank. He himself survived a gas attack in France, and the snobbery of some at Magdalen which had a reputation of being a rich man's college.

Denning was appointed to the bench near the end of the World War II. He started in divorce. He was not familiar with it, so he went to Somerset House to look at a decree nisi. He used to do fifty undefended divorces a day, and he did not give one reserved judgment in his first twelve months. He almost immediately came under notice as an innovative lawyer with a judgment – given 'off the reel' – that revived the doctrine of equity precluding people going back on their word in respect of the effect of their contract. He also wrote prolifically and soon became the darling of law students, and teachers, throughout the common law world.

Denning was the Master of the Rolls, the head of the Court of Appeal in England, for twenty years. In that time he redefined the way in which judgments were written in England and elsewhere. He had a remarkable capacity to state facts simply and then the law with apparently just as much simplicity. Although he was idolised by academia, he was distrusted by the old guard on the bench. He was from time to time criticised, if not savaged, by more conservative lawyers, particularly Lord Simonds. 'I, too, was ambitious. I, too, was accused of heresy – and verbally beheaded, by Lord Simonds.'

Denning was protected in his reputation as a radical innovator because this very old-fashioned Englishman, and man of the Church of England, was rarely exposed to crime, industrial relations, race relations or morals generally. If he had been let loose in those fields, he would have lost a lot of points with his admirers.

Holmes had admired the way that the English Court of Appeal dealt with appeals on the spot. Denning continued that tradition. When Denning presided over the Court of Appeal, it heard about 800 cases a year (about the number decided by Lord Mansfield). About fifty or sixty reached the ultimate court, the House of Lords. The Court sat five days a week, all day. Only about one case in ten was reserved. Judgments had to be written at the weekend. Only recently has the court stopped sitting on Fridays. Some said that when he was made a Lord, Denning wrote to the College of Arms requesting palm trees on his coat of arms. He has often been subjected to that kind of criticism, but it is impossible to find any appellate court in the common law world today operating with the degree of speed, efficiency, rigour, and sheer juristic horse-power, as that over which Denning presided. We are only talking of a distance of one generation.

Even at this distance in time and, for some of us, space, it is still breathtaking to watch the likes of Mansfield, Holmes and Denning at work. For the rest of us, it is like travelling along the freeway at a fast clip, and being conscious of a Rolls Royce slipping quietly past and realising that it has a lot more left in the tank.

To go back to where we started in this chapter, you can only understand the law by learning of those who made it. But perhaps also we might try to learn where we have gone wrong by seeing where those in the past got it right. In bringing ourselves up to our own time, we have passed over the great reforms of the 19th century. They were tragically overdue. We must not forget the frightful mess that the common law had got into. The courts literally stank. Dickens savaged them in novels like *Bleak House* and *Pickwick Papers*. In the Storrs Lectures at Yale, Holdsworth endorsed Dickens. For example, he said of Chancery that 'it was the contrast between the smug complacency and respectability of the court, and the ruin which it brought upon all persons and things which it got within its grasp, which inspired Dickens's pen'. Unfortunately, smug complacency and respectability are occupational hazards for courts.

X
Law and Morals

> Wealth, in a commercial age, is made up largely of promises.
> *Roscoe Pound*

Many lawyers believe that the law has nothing to do with morals, but in reviewing its history, we have often seen the impact of our moral code on our laws.

Let us take crime first. We should go first to our criminal law, because it came first in the development of our Anglo-Saxon law, and because there is not much point in having the world's best practice laws of financial securities if we do not have an effective law against murder. The laws of our Godless German ancestors relating to murder and theft – mainly cattle-stealing – were not expressed in moral terms, even if they were driven by moral views. But gradually our common law evolved to the stage – reached many centuries ago – where its starting point was that there is no crime unless there is a guilty mind. The Latin maxim said that the act was not guilty – that is, a crime – unless the mind was guilty.

The requirement of a guilty mind might be translated into intention to kill (in murder) or intention to deprive someone permanently of property (in theft), but what matters is that our law turned its face away from what we call strict liability for crime, that is, a crime which is constituted by the prohibited act whatever may have been the state of mind of the accused. We believe that if the government wants to take your life or liberty from you, it must prove that you have breached a law and that you did so with a guilty mind. In ordinary language, the government must show that you are morally guilty because you did something that was morally wrong. We do not expect to hear a judge say 'I find you guilty of theft although I am quite satisfied that your action was honest.'

So, even in medieval times, a guilty act alone would not establish guilt at law if, for example, you were only ten, or you were out of your mind and did not know what you were doing, or if you had been coerced into doing what you did by participants in a civil war during a complete breakdown of public authority.

It is obvious that the punishment inflicted by the law for crimes will vary with the degree of moral guilt. As more court time is spent assessing sentence than determining guilt, the preoccupation with morals is inevitable. But we still find moral guilt essential to the definition of many crimes. You can still find in the books an offence of 'cheating the Crown'.

If you knowingly make a false statement to the tax people for the purposes of financial gain, you might on a bad day be charged with theft. If you or your lawyer get together to plan to get your tax down dishonestly, you might both be charged with conspiring to defraud the revenue. Then your new lawyers will have your complete attention when they tell you that the Crown has only to prove three things: an agreement (a matter of fact); that was unlawful (a matter of law for the judge); and that your conduct was *dishonest*. This last is a question for the jury, and it is an issue on which they will get alarmingly little instruction from the judge. How many lawyers would not be alarmed to have their professional conduct scrutinised by ordinary people according to their ordinary bring-your-own views of dishonesty?

This was the position of the common law – the law made by the judges – but the laws made by the parliaments have tended to proceed differently. The shift back to strict liability was understandable on issues of workers' rights and public safety, but the continuing dilution or deletion of the need for moral guilt is not helping to maintain public respect for our criminal law.

The greatest judge that this country has produced gave two responses to the growth of strict liability for crime. Sir Owen Dixon said that if you interpreted some of these 'strict' statutory crimes correctly, they might reveal a defence if the person charged could show 'an honest and reasonable belief' in a state of facts which would have taken the accused out of the operation of the statute (*Proudman v Dayman*). If the parliament could take 'honesty' out of the offence, perhaps the judges could bring it back in via the defence.

Then the English judges said that in certain common law offences, a criminal intent might be not just inferred, but presumed, so that the Crown did not have to prove it. This was too much for Dixon, and Australia severed the ties that had been so lovingly preserved with the mother country. The High Court said that it was 'seldom helpful and always dangerous' to suggest that a man is presumed to intend the consequences of his act (*Parker v R*).

This was a very big break – it was almost exciting. It is hard to find a similar example since then of our courts taking a firm stand on principle against ill-considered and unnecessary incursions from above.

Putting the criminal law to one side, what about that part of the law that says that we are obliged to act carefully towards others, or to compensate those who are hurt by our failure to be careful? This is the civil wrong of *negligence*. It does not make sense to most people to say that we are under a duty not to murder, rape, or steal, but it does make sense to say that we have a moral duty when driving a car to drive carefully so that we do not by our lack of care expose others to an unnecessary risk of injury. The moral duty is easy to understand. It may proceed through a civil duty and give rise to a criminal liability. If I go through red lights when drunk and kill someone, my want of care for others should see me in gaol for many years.

But how were the judges to distinguish between the two? When would the law say that I have a duty to take care to avoid hurting others which would make me liable to compensate the victim but not to go to gaol? Oliver Wendell Holmes said that both the criminal law and the law of civil wrongs 'started from a moral basis, from the thought that someone was to blame'. Both history and experience suggest that this is still the case – at least at common law. The relevant duty might be circumscribed by policy or economics, but its origin is moral.

In the leading US case, an injured driver (who was not the first purchaser) sued the manufacturer of Buick cars. The car crashed when a wooden wheel failed. The car was designed to do 50 miles per hour. This led Cardozo, J to remark that 'unless its wheels were sound and strong, injury was almost certain'. The Court said it would not stay locked in the horse and buggy age – while the principles did not change, the rules had to be cast to meet 'whatever the needs of life in a developing civilisation required them to be' (*MacPherson v Buick Motor Co*). Meeting the needs of civilization is a large aspiration.

In the UK case a woman, who had not bought the offending product, took ill in the presence of a decomposing snail in a soft drink. Lord Atkin, like Cardozo, J, referred to the precedents before stating the duty of care in much broader terms than had been used before. Lord Atkin defined the duty not just by morality, but also by Scripture – the Sermon on the Mount. His Lordship saw his task as being to say who was his 'neighbour' as a matter of law (*Donoghue v Stevenson*).

Now, since those two decisions, the law has moved steadily away from the stark moral simplicity and intellectual honesty of each of them. It is very hard to see how any part of that movement has been in any way beneficial. What we get may remind us of the play of Pirandello, *Six Characters in Search of an Author*.

If I make a promise I should keep it. That is a moral proposition but, allowing for exceptions, people who are not amoral accept it. If you behave so that you may be said to have gone back on your word or reneged on a deal, you have let yourself down morally. People think less of you.

A contract is a promise (or agreement) that the law enforces. But the law does not enforce all promises. Does this mean that the law has no concern with the moral value of people keeping their promises? Of course not – the second proposition does not follow from the first. If I promise to reward every athlete who runs a mile in less than four minutes, I am encouraging athletics. My encouragement may be limited, but that does not mean that it does not exist. The law may enforce only some promises, but it remains the case that the law enforces those promises because people believe morally that promises should be kept. If I go into the Army, I remain a citizen; if I cease to be a sergeant and become an officer, I remain a soldier. We should not allow labels to extinguish reality. We should maintain our respect for the given word.

The wealth of nations consists largely of promises, or the expectation that those promises will be met. In assessing that wealth, the moral value underlying those promises hardly matters. But as between John and Betty, a promise – to marry for example – has a moral worth, and no other – its legal value does not matter (and it may be nil). The French Code stipulated that a legal agreement took the place of the law for those who made it – but the supervening law did not sterilize the original moral bond.

Why does the law not enforce all of the promises that we regard as morally binding, or binding in honour, what some call gentlemen's agreements? If I promise to mow the lawns of the widow next door and then renege, for no good reason, should she be able to take me to court and get the judge to order me to mow her lawns or to pay compensation for the higher amount charged by my successor? If this instance resembles what the police might term a 'domestic' matter, do we want our world to be so regimented that the court may intervene in my affairs every time I have a falling out with one of my neighbours or a member of my family?

The law proceeds on the footing that the answer is no. But what if the widow agrees to pay me $100 a week in return for my promise to mow her lawns? This now looks like a commercial transaction. What if I have bought a new mower and given up my day job in reliance on the agreement? Would it be fair to allow the widow to

Laws and Morals

cancel the deal without accounting to me? No – and even a widow can lose a lawsuit.

These, then, are the filters that the judges apply before allowing the law to be invoked to enforce the moral value of a promise. They look to see whether the parties intended to enforce their arrangement, and they look to see some benefit provided or cost incurred by the party seeking to enforce the arrangement. You have to earn the right to enforce a promise in court. This is what the law calls *consideration*.

But whether the promise is legally enforceable or not, the underlying moral premise is the same. People in business who use legal technicalities to escape their obligations, and the basic premise that my word is my bond are, to put it softly, not well regarded.

Practising lawyers often find that the two hardest questions put to them are these: 'Have I done enough to lock Betty in to this arrangement legally?', and 'Has Betty done enough wrong to let me walk away from the deal and say all bets are off?' The questions are frequently hard for the court, but it is idle to suggest that the moral view is completely irrelevant, even if it may be said to be in theory unmentionable.

I do the lawns and the widow says she does not have the money: she was robbed (or she lost her money at the poker machines). Does this matter? Morally, yes; legally, no. A promise is a promise and the court is not inclined to rewrite contracts to respond to the dictate of accidents of history.

Someone steals my lawn mower. Is there any difference here to the widow losing her money? No. The widow's property is destroyed by fire and there is no lawn left to mow. Now the court is on firm ground to intervene to excuse the widow (if I was miserable enough to complain). The court would rule that the widow was discharged because it was physically impossible for the contract to be performed. A literary judge might even refer to a Latin poet: 'It was not unto this contract that I came'.

So, it is inevitable that moral considerations will underlie the resolution of disputes under agreements between people. Justice Holmes said: 'The duty to keep a contract at common law means a prediction that you must pay damages if you do not keep it – and nothing else'. This cold New England dogma may or may not represent the law, but few people would think that the law is the end of the matter. Let us put to one side those contracts – like sales of land – that the court may order to be carried out on pain of a term in gaol for contempt. If Betty enters into one of those agreements that the law will enforce, what do we think of Betty if she calmly sits down and assesses which option is better for her – going through with the deal and being as good as her word, or welshing and telling the other side that she will see them in court if they are good enough?

Sadly, something like that hard attitude underlies some major corporates who have the power to wear down most complainants and who have people to tell them that the margins are worth it. And, together with nastiness and greed, they have been helped to reach this revolting position – rather like that reached by the German judiciary after 1936 – that their obligations are to be found in their laws, and nowhere else. Whatever may have been the case in some European societies in the past, or in some Asian regimes now, it is beyond argument for us that people who limit their moral obligations to those stated in their published laws are not to be trusted and are morally deprived.

So, the moral value of a promise underlies the legal value of a bargain, and it is the bargain – the law prefers the word 'contract' – that underlies most of our law of property, employment, industrial relations, banking, insurance, insolvency and trade. Some members of the community would be surprised to be told that bankers or insurers owe them a moral obligation. They do, but the moral obligation is overlaid by the legal, to the point of extinction. Apart from drenching the obligations in the contract, we have drenched the corporation itself with layers and layers of legal obligations. Not surprisingly, the corporates say that if a question is not dealt with by the black letter of the law or by the very words of the contract, then there is no obligation upon them. The game comes down to one of them and their money against the world.

Laws and Morals

After the great San Francisco earthquake, a famous underwriter, Cuthbert Heath, sent a telegram saying that he would honour all claims regardless of the wording of the policy. You would not see that now. Sadly, you would see exactly the opposite. People of the City were once respected because they kept their word. The law must share the blame for their decline.

Firms define the rights of their stakeholders and their managers by the contracts between them as supplemented by the law. It is the same with their employees – you start with the contract. This model is followed in constitutional documents between the components of a federation. Companies record the agreement between shareholders and directors in a document like articles of association. The constitution of states and federal bodies record the anterior compact between governing entities and their citizens, and this agreement is embodied in a statute of fundamental importance. When the US wanted to break away from the UK, Jefferson wrote a long lawyer's letter saying that the British Crown had repudiated its agreement with the American colonies, which were therefore entitled to be discharged from that agreement and say that it was at an end. This was the Declaration of Independence.

It is obvious that one reason why we lose sight of morality in actions on contracts is that we have too much law. Simple moral propositions are disguised or buried. What might be called the primacy of contract, the supremacy of the bargain, has been further eroded by, ironically, the largest avenue for importing morality directly into the law – the law that we call equity.

It has been the role of equity, and it still is, to afford comfort where justice demands it, either because the law is too narrow or because it is too hard – either the law has no remedy, or because its remedy does not meet the requirements of fairness in a given case. If you ask most people if there is any difference between the requirements of morality and the requirements of conscience, they might give you a long look, but very few would say that conscience does not reach as far as morality.

Is it the law, then, that our judges can put the law aside when their conscience tells them? Of course not: the judges are right to say that they are not courts of conscience. We have buried our equity with as much regulation by precedent as we have buried our law of contract. But we have allowed people to succeed in actions on a contract where, as a matter of law, there was none. The judges have done this where they think that it would be unfair – or unjust or unconscionable, but never 'immoral' – to allow one party to go back on their word because the other party has relied on it. You can see how this approach might make consideration unnecessary.

Problems must arise when conscience is allowed to run over the law in business. The ethereal does not mix with the fiscal and, if nothing else, predictability goes down. The Romans had similar problems. Their equity went further than ours. Roman equity could relieve from the consequences not just of fraud, mistake, accident, oppression or hardship – but from subtlety (*subtilitas*). Now, that looks to be a valuable weapon to have in your arsenal against lawyers who are too clever to be trusted – too crafty, even. But what do you do if you find that the lawyers who are the cleverest and the most subtle are the lawyers who practise in that body of law that we describe as equity?

If I undertake to hold property on trust for another, I have a moral duty to give effect to that trust. Since these undertakings began with land in medieval Europe – we are not just talking of mowing the lawns, but of the land itself – the law could only have refused to enforce these undertakings by making itself irrelevant and generating an underground system of title. Well, the law did not make itself irrelevant, but it did generate an underground system of title by enforcing *trusts* through a different body of law than that used to enforce contracts. The results have been pleasing to those who like patchwork quilts and not paying tax, but not so pleasing to those who want to secure their loans (and so need to see everything on the table) and those who have to pay tax.

This dual system of interests in property – some legally registrable, others not; above the table, and under the table – continually generates a faculty in our law that some practitioners celebrate for all the wrong reasons – subtlety. Just as the subtleties of philosophy have taken the Church away from the simple faith of the Sermon on the Mount, so the subtleties of equity have taken our courts away from the simple faith of the moral precepts on which our common law stands.

If I undertake to act in the interests of Bob, I should honour my undertaking. Bob has put his trust and confidence in me to look after his interests, not my own, and if my interests get in the way, I should tell him. If I seize a chance that comes my way while looking after Bob to make a profit for myself, then, whether or not Bob could have taken the opportunity, I should account to him for what I have gained. These moral precepts are simple enough. They apply as much to a boy on a paper round as to the man who makes the papers, Mr Rupert Murdoch.

But it damages our claim to have a mature, stable system of law that these moral duties are imported into basic contractual arrangements by the same body of law that has led to dual land ownership. Do we have two moralities? If Bob agrees to run a boarding-school, Bob knows that he is there to look after the students, not to molest them; if Bob agrees to act as a director of a company, he knows he is there to make profits for shareholders, not for himself; Bob needs no contract or statute, no lawyer or bureaucrat, to tell him of the minimal requirements of human decency.

Over the last generation or so, a whole new body of law has been recognised under the rubric of 'unjust enrichment'. Now, you might think that you could hardly get a law more rooted in morality than one that says that you might have to suffer if you get unjustly enriched – just see how pregnant with moralizing is each of those loaded words: a law against *injustice*! a law against *enrichment*! – but it is an excommunicable heresy to suggest that this bounteous law derives from *equity*.

The basic moral rules are often restated in parliament. People in business should avoid conduct that is 'misleading or deceptive'. Their transactions are at risk if they have been 'unconscionable'. Corporations must not be 'predatory'. If there is a dispute amongst stakeholders, the court may wind the business up on grounds that are 'just and equitable'. The same goes if the majority has been 'oppressive'. Directors and other employees have to act 'honestly' and for a 'proper purpose'. A testator with dependants or others with a 'moral claim' has to make 'adequate' and 'proper' provision for them. You do not find any of these direct, but broad, moral imperatives in the Code of Hammurabi, the Twelve Tablets, or the Laws of Solon. But we have also drenched the moral precepts in black letter detail that would have signified madness to the ancients.

Yet we still feel lost when shifted too far from our moral base. One of the reasons that specialist areas of the law like tax, industrial relations, planning, or divorce, lack appeal for those who do not practise in them is that to outsiders they do not appear to have a safe moral bedrock, sometimes with the result that they appear to be just as bereft intellectually.

The part of our law that appears to have the least to do with morals may have the most. We reserve the grand title of 'constitutional' for the law that says how our governments are to live together. Administrative law deals with how governments relate to their subjects. When it deals with how courts must behave, our common law deals with what others put in Bills of Rights. (The English *Bill of Rights* is part of our general law, but that is another matter).

The law says that judges have to hear both sides, and must not be prejudiced. This part of our law, developed over a thousand years, is part of what we call the Rule of Law. What is its premise? All people must as a matter of law be treated as equal before the law. Just as we would prefer to have some who are guilty go free rather than innocents be sent to gaol, so we think that people count for more than political ideas.

All these rubrics are held together by the common law. What holds it together? The doctrine of precedent. If you have two children and you give one a bigger present, or a tougher penalty, than the other, then stand back and watch the poison do its work and watch the disaffection set in. Even a dog, it is said, knows the difference between being kicked deliberately and being kicked accidentally. The need for equal, consistent treatment, for symmetry, runs very, very deep. We apply to the denial of the right to fairness epithets like arbitrary, capricious, and tyrannical, and we brand the regimes we least admire with just that denial.

That like cases should be treated alike is a proposition that would not occur to a fascist dictator or an absolute sheikh, neither of whom would have any idea of the rule of law, but for us it is fundamental. Whether we regard it as moral or not – and it certainly looks moral – may not matter much. It is presupposed – that is, it is taken for granted or as a given – in our whole understanding of the operation of law and justice. It is axiomatic to our law that like cases must be treated alike, just as it is axiomatic to our logic that a thing cannot both be and not be at the same time. The price of denying either is taking yourself out of the game.

What are the moral rules we have referred to? Do not hurt others. Do not steal. Be careful not to hurt others accidentally. If you make a promise or give an undertaking, honour it. Do not seek gain by deceit. If you agree to look after another, look after that person and not yourself. If you accept an office, do so faithfully. People should be treated fairly, equally, and according to the rules.

What are the sources of these rules? As it happens, most people here would subscribe to them in one form or another and that, in itself, is enough to establish their moral authority. Each may derive ultimately from what is called the Golden Rule, that we should behave as we would wish others to behave. Variations of this rule can be found in both the Old and New Testaments. The secular version is in Kant, and may be expressed as: 'Act as if the maxim of your action were to become through you a universal law.'

It is entirely natural that lawyers, including judges in particular, should be shy about allowing moral views to colour and then distort legal opinions. Judges have enough to do on the Bench without colliding with government or God. But it is also dangerous to allow legal opinions to form in a moral vacuum. Rape is rape; welshing is welshing; and smarties are smarties. The basic rules of law give effect to basic moral values. There is nothing shameful or odd about that, or about the fact that judges and lawyers live in the world. The once fashionable posture for judges of unworldliness is no longer good enough. It was well and truly dead before Leo McKern, as Rumpole on television, left us.

The time has also passed when judges felt able to reach a decision that was an insult to the moral views of the community and then just pretend that they were just doing their job and that no one got hurt. That time passed in the early 1980s when the courts realised the very great damage they were doing to the faith of the public by upholding artificial tax schemes. They had done so by applying literally the black letter of the law with a veneer of misplaced technicality that violated the sense of decency – both intellectual and moral – of those members of the community who paid their taxes, but who did not have the privilege of being invested with the same level of subtlety as those ermine clad champions of the rich.

And finally there are the lessons of experience. Lawyers who go to court day in and day out intrinsically understand the truth of the observation of Roscoe Pound that 'analytical jurists grossly underestimated the role of morals in everyday decisions'. Dean Pound had learned this truth the hard way. He used to appear before cow-punching juries in Nebraska – for the railroad companies, who could never be in the right. But it is not just the case of a widow against a bank, or of seeing off a dud technical point. Lawyers coming into a case instinctively feel for *the* legal issue, but just as strongly they seek to get a feel for who has *the merits* – the moral high ground. There is frequently cross-party agreement on this, even though unexpressed, and it forms the basis of settlement discussions and, as often as not, the decision.

The simple truth is that moral views play a significant role in practice in the disposal of litigation, and the greater the technicality of the law, the more important will be the part that morals play in resolving issues arising under it.

Laws and Morals

The time for keeping the law simple has long passed. Many believe that the time for making the law understandable or even manageable, has also passed. But we might at least try to keep it decent. We are not keeping faith with our history; if we manage to lose touch with our morals, the game will be well and truly up.

XI
Actual Decline and Likely Fall

Judges are forbidden, when giving judgment in the cases which are brought before them, to lay down general rules of conduct or decide a case by holding it was governed by previous decisions.

(*Code Napoleon*, Article 5)

For it is always to be remembered that justice is made up of individual cases. If the judicial machinery does not produce speedy, inexpensive and just results in the actual cases that pass through it, no amount of mechanical or theoretical perfection will atone.

(*Roscoe Pound*)

Common law as case law is the product of conflict, but the common law itself has appeared to thrive on conflicts that it has created. We have seen a conflict between common law and equity; common law and civil (Roman) law; and common law and statute law. As practised in those jurisdictions that follow the British model, there is still a division, and consequent conflict, between barristers and solicitors. The cast of mind of the common law does not handle well the absolutes of a binding constitution. The English, it appears, distrust dogma as much as they distrust philosophy.

There is a thread of humaneness that runs through the common law that we would be foolish to forget and wrong to repudiate. Those

Actual Decline and Likely Fall

who smile at such a broad but fond proposition may care to nominate which jurisdictions they think do it better.

But there is also a thread of individualism. We saw Maitland talking of the English judge as being like the umpire at a cricket match. Dean Wigmore would in the 20th century refer to 'the sporting theory of justice' – the idea that the judicial administration of justice is a game to be played to the bitter end. This notion was given full play in the US with its frontier attitude to litigation and the law and the distrust of the Puritans for the softness of equity. Equity helps fools out of bad bargains they had made for themselves. Hence the reluctance of Massachusetts – the home state of Holmes – to grant equity powers to its courts.

The Puritans had a jealousy of the judge that went with an objection to individualisation in the criminal law that was tied to their revulsion for the Star Chamber. But even before coming to the Puritans – who were, after all, able to get their own way in New England – Roscoe Pound saw that the individualism of the common law came from its beginning with the strict old Germanic law. This law 'insisted that every man should stand upon his own two feet and should play the game as a man, without squealing …' Pound was qualified to talk of the influence of the Puritans and the frontier. He came from long lines of Quakers and was born only seven years after the first log cabin was put up in Indian country that became Lincoln, Nebraska. His parents' wedding trip out West took eight days; they crossed the Missouri by ice. Pound recalled appearing for a railway company that was the plaintiff – and lo! he won. He sought out a juror who told him the judge had tried to trick them – the judge had said that the railroad was the plaintiff; but they knew better and gave the plaintiff a good verdict to 'soak the railroad' in any event. There you have a story that shows how whole libraries cannot supply the knowledge got in court.

This sort of 'coming ready or not' attitude of the common law will not sit well with paternalist intervention from either the Chancery or the Parliament, and the lingering distrust of and distaste for both is one of the factors in the catalogue of problems of the common law that we will look to in closing.

Sclerosis

We are slowly drowning in laws of a volume and complexity that would have been unimaginable to those whose writings we have been considering. For example, barely 150 years ago, Sir Henry Maine said: 'Legislation has nearly confessed its inability to keep pace with the activity of man in discovery, in invention, and in the manipulation of accumulated wealth.' Holmes said: 'Any legal standard must in theory be capable of being known – the defendant is supposed to know the law.' Nearly a century ago, Pound said that the common law in the US had survived 'the huge mass of legislation that is placed annually upon our statute books and gives to it form and consistency'.

We saw that the final phase of legal history identified by Maine was Legislation. Next came as part of the same phase Socialization. There the interest shifted to the interests of society rather than the rights of the individual. The phase we are in now may be called Sclerosis. We might define it for legal purposes as a disease associated with aging that involves a thickening and hardening of channels which in turn impairs circulation and which in the event of a blockage may be fatal.

The great fictions of the modern law include: 'I understand corporations laws'; 'I understand my tax filing'; 'I understand my board's response to the takeover offer'; 'I know the difference between fiduciaries and merchants'; 'I know what predatory pricing is'; and so on.

What has this to do with the common law? Well, as Pound remarked, if the common lawyers refuse to act intelligently, they can expect the unintelligent reaction from the legislative steamroller. Common lawyers do not react well to legislation. They regard it as a bureaucratic intrusion on their turf, sponsored by people who do not know what they are talking about. Questions of statutory interpretation engage our appellate courts now for most of their time, but they still approach these cases like common law cases. They write long judgments as if

Actual Decline and Likely Fall

they were making the law, and not simply clarifying it. There is no reason why statutory questions should not be disposed of in a page or two, like clarifying a train time-table. The reasoning will not be used to support a new law, because it is the parliament that is making the law, not the court that is clarifying it.

This is also part of the problem. Judges think that it is a good idea to report judgments to make new law. Nothing could be further from the truth. We have too much already. Take the law of contract. This is fundamental to business and capitalism. It is in essence simple enough to state. There are two questions that trouble commercial lawyers all the time. When have the parties gone from negotiation to a binding contract? When has one misbehaved enough to allow the other to say that it is all over? The relevant law can be stated in a few pages, but the lawyer knows that it is not the law as written that counts, but rather the skill and nerve of the lawyer. The standard text book on contract in the United States is *Williston*. It currently runs to 31 volumes. The judges complain about the number of laws made by parliaments, but they are no better, and the long lectures read by appellate courts to trial judges just mean that their jobs get harder, and then the lectures get even longer.

We have known for a while that we have too much law, and too much inept law, and that one day business will simply collapse under the weight of the law. But the law just keeps getting worse on a daily basis, and there is no reason at all to believe that we can reverse the process and get out of this mess by lawful use of the democratic process. We are in too deep with too much riding on the system – such as currencies, banks, and stock exchanges – for us to disentangle it or do anything other than just wait to see what survives the inevitable collapse. We have succeeded in doing to the law what we may have succeeded in doing to the planet – we have loaded it up with so much refuse that it is choking to death.

Is it not plain enough that each time that a parliament or a court makes a new law, these consequences follow as night the day – the law is increased, and with it is increased the chance that the law will not be found, understood, or complied with, but will be breached and then argued over, with all the attendant troubles?

As for the judges who want to keep making unnecessary laws, they may reflect on the observation of Holmes:

> When a man has a working knowledge of his business, he can spend his leisure better than in reading all the reported cases he has time for. They are apt to be only the small change of legal thought.

If this book has said anything, it is that the common law is made by people who try and decide cases, not by people who sit and deliver opinions. We pay judges, and we pay them handsomely, to decide cases, not to build monuments to what they fondly see as jurisprudence. If the judges do their job, the rest follows. The code words are 'incremental', 'interstitial' and 'accretion'. If judges want to be scholars they can get a job in another part of town. As well as handing over their wigs, they will have to take what is called a haircut – about two thirds. Real scholars have never been overpaid.

Schizophrenia

Equity split off from the medieval common law when it was primitively formal, but we have still not been able to put the two back together again. You would think that about 700 years would allow the children to recover from the divorce, especially since the cure of equity became worse than the disease of the common law.

It is no answer to say that the Chancery did some good. The English courts were hardly going to go for nearly a millennium without developing the necessary remedies. It is not to the point whether subpoenas or injunctions are to be called 'equitable' or 'Martian'. We have seen that people asked for a 'fair go' outside of the law by going straight to the regal source, and that the original writ of covenant looks very like a decree of specific performance in equity. Why now should someone asking for an injunction have to argue now that the common law – damages – is not good enough?

Actual Decline and Likely Fall

Why does my stockbroker have to act in good faith to me while I do not have to act in good faith to my banker?

Are we talking about anything other than overcoming the effect of accidents of history? What reason is there, *a priori*, to postulate that the law of trusts and the process of injunction rather than the law of larceny and the process of arrest should turn on issues of conscience determined by the judges in the Chancery part of the royal judicature?

You can understand the suspicion that some have of equity when you reflect, as did the Puritans, on 'equity' being invoked in the criminal law. Imagine now if a criminal court claimed an 'equity' to deal with misconduct that the judges thought had escaped the strict application of the law. Such a principle is warmly embraced by revolutionary tribunals and totalitarian courts, but not in the common law (notwithstanding the decision in *DPP v Shaw*.) You can understand how macabre might be the consequence of equity entering the common law from an exchange in the trial of Walter Raleigh. Raleigh told the Court that 'your Lordships, as ministers of the King, are bound to administer the law in equity.' Coke replied: 'Equity must proceed from the King; you can only have justice from us'.

Of course, the common law did have a safety valve for softening the rigour of the law relating to crimes, but it came from the jury, not from the Chancery. In Elizabethan times, jurors were sworn to give a verdict according to their conscience, and in ancient Athens they swore 'to vote according to the laws where there are laws, and where there is not, to vote as justly as in us lies.'

A person holding a position of trust might expect to be sued for breaching that trust. But if the claim is one for compensation for damage arising from the breach of trust – probably called a breach of fiduciary duty – there might be a long argument turning on English legislation during the reign of Queen Victoria about the nature of the right to recover damages. The same would be the case where someone seeks to profit from using information that they know to be confidential. In either case, if the person sued is a company director, the damages may be measured in millions. There may also be issues about exemplary damages (for which the director will not be insured) which depend on whether the right being asserted is characterised as 'legal' or 'equitable'. The directors may then have their houses riding on an issue that to them looks like it will be resolved by reference to Tarot cards.

The failure of the lawyers to get their act together on the 'fusion' of law and equity is a sad case of a misspent regard for history. It is also a failure of intellect and will, and it is often seen at its worst in those former colonies where the notion of a Court of Conscience might seem as odd as that of a club for gentlemen. The judgment of Maitland now stands more generally for us.

> Freed from contact with the plain man in the jury-box, the Chancellors were tempted to forget how plain and rough good law should be, and to screw up the legal standard of reasonable conduct to a height hardly attainable except by those whose purses could command the constant advice of a family solicitor. A court which started with the idea of doing summary justice for the poor became a court which did a highly refined, but tardy, justice suitable only to the rich.

Delay

Well before Hamlet complained of the law's delay, Fortescue had asked why the process took so much longer in England than elsewhere. The answer was what we still get today. 'Justice is never so safe when the process is hurried on.' Ours is a superior product.

The trouble was and is that justice delayed is justice denied. Both are in breach of the Great Charter.

You can find delay in three phases – getting the case to trial, getting through the trial, and then getting judgment. Eldon was notorious on all three, but for the most part now the delay is in getting to trial or in the length of the trial. The problem in each case is a failure by the judges properly to manage the process, or, nowadays, by managing it too much in some jurisdictions. It is common for there to be an argument

Actual Decline and Likely Fall

between the judges and the executive as to who is responsible, but ultimately the judges have to answer for the justice that they provide.

The old rules about pleading are either not understood or not properly enforced to narrow the issue to one that a jury could give an answer on (which is what they were built for). The equity process of discovery has got out of hand almost entirely across the common law world, and the bastard merged but not 'fused' process has put a lot of litigation beyond the reach of the courts, let alone the litigants.

The excessive time taken by the trial itself is partly caused by the lack of hard trial experience in too many lawyers and judges, and partly by a reluctance by the judges to impose time limits. If it is good enough for the United States Supreme Court, the most powerful court on earth, why is it not good enough for trial courts? Part of the problem is also the complexity of the law and the fear of trial judges of not being supported on appeal. We have also widened the ambit of inquiry into, say, contract cases. Previously, if a contract was in writing, our ancestors would not let the parties go outside the writing. Now, we find all sorts of ways of doing just that, and what would have been a half day case now takes a week.

The speed of trials in the past comes as a shock to us now. Put to one side the trials of Socrates and Jesus that we referred to in the first chapter. The great treason trials in which Coke appeared by convention each finished in one day. Take the Nuremberg trials – war crimes, the trial of European civilization, and multiple hangings. They took less than a year. (The military tribunal limited each accused to one day for the final address of his lawyer) The trial of O.J. Simpson for murder – a tawdry if partly televised domestic – took 133 days. They teach you at Harvard that trial lawyers do not know how to run Class Actions now because they are so big that they must all settle. This problem is general now.

Judges, particularly appellate judges, have been frightened out of giving judgment on the spot. This could be done in cases of appeals on sentence or statutory interpretation. How long does it take to say 'I am not God'? All appeals should require special leave. Appeals are forms of litigation meant to extend litigation, and should not be encouraged. If the judges are to prescribe how trial judges work, they should make rules requiring judgments after trials to be given promptly – within, say, four weeks at the outside. Among other things, trial judges might then be encouraged to dispose of litigation rather than prepare some dim claim to immortality which looks like a submission to *The Harvard Law Review* and is the last thing on earth that either party might wish to sponsor, and which may well, after all, fall into the category of 'the small change'.

Truth

While a common law trial is not a quest for absolute truth, proceedings in equity may look more like such a quest. They did resemble more the inquisitorial model – the evidence was in writing; it was accumulated over time in something like a dossier; and the force of the State was applied to determine the state of the conscience of the party whose conduct was in question. The resultant findings and decree are worlds away from a simple verdict in a case of murder or negligence (the verdict in each case being inscrutable). It is as far away as the decree of Chancery was from the conclusion of a trial by battle or ordeal.

Yet we mix all these functions up in our merged process. There is nothing wrong with mixing up processes of the common law and equity, but it helps if we remember how and why they were devised. A little history may be informative.

Our law was for us unbelievably primitive when we did not allow the accused or the parties to give evidence on their own behalf. But what would our ancestors think of our practice of allowing the lawyers to give evidence on behalf of their clients? This is what we in substance permit when lawyers are involved in preparing written statements to be tendered in evidence, whether those statements are sworn (as was the practice in Chancery) or not. Some jurisdictions permitted the accused in a criminal trial to make an unsworn statement. This practice was wound up because too many lawyers could not be trusted to play the game according to the rules and leave it up to the client to provide the substance of the statement. How would we react today if a lawyer went into the box and said that she would take examination-in-chief on behalf of her client and then allow the client to be cross-examined? The idea of a written statement would be unthinkable before a jury, and should be unthinkable before any other tribunal of fact. The determined continuance of this pernicious practice of flirting with the truth is in part a consequence of our surrendering of the right to a trial by jury. How can a tribunal of fact proceed in good conscience to give a verdict on competing versions of history when it has only heard witnesses cross-examined and it has denied them the right to present their version in chief? Their evidence is either contested or not; if the latter, it need not be in writing; if the former, it should not be. Has any common lawyer with trial experience ever sought to argue the contrary? Has anyone involved in hearing cases for a quarter of a century expressed a different view?

While we allow litigants to skirt around the truth with our equity process, we allow them to seek to convert a trial of a simple issue at common law into an inquiry about the character of the parties through the process of discovery. It was devised to get at the conscience of the parties sued. It is now mainly invoked against parties that have no conscience, fictitious legal persons that we call companies. One problem is that like tax returns, the discovery system is based on the honour system. The directors of corporate parties are rarely personally involved. The members of management who are put forward to put their names to the process will have consciences – but in Chancery the process was backed by the sanction of the oath when that meant as much for the medieval deponent as an actual threat of being blasted in eternal fires. Such threats that the system now has are not likely to outweigh the implicit risk of the loss of a job if the management person singled out to take the flak makes a bad career choice. The same goes for a lot of the lawyers at the big end of town.

Rightly or wrongly, we have come a long way from the distant and aloof cricket umpire of Maitland. The one sad truth that appears to emerge is that the more the judges involve themselves in the process before and at trial, the longer it seems to take, and the more expensive it gets.

Misgovernment

The Westminster system is disintegrating. Essential to it was the notion of responsible government. Ministers were responsible to the parliament for the acts of civil servants in the folios that they were in charge of. It was also essential that the civil service was to be politically independent and have appropriate security of tenure. These usages were customary and they have been allowed simply to disappear through disuse. We will come back to juries, but here simply notice that one of the checks on government power, at last as important as the writ of Habeas Corpus for at least the last 600 years or so has been trial by jury. We are losing this, too.

Status

The heyday of freedom of contract came in Victorian England. It was inevitable and desirable that the parliament or the courts should intervene to protect those who needed protecting. The workers were the first and most obvious case, after married women. Later came consumers and shareholders and traders who needed protection from predators. It is not of itself a bad thing that as a result of these laws, people may find that their rights depend upon their status rather than what they have managed to achieve through a contract.

The problem with status now is at the other end. How do we control those corporations that have such might and power that they think they can walk over anyone, including the government, and do what they like?

It is here that the Americans are well ahead of the rest. There are four reasons. The Americans pioneered the use of class actions and have used them as an instrument of social engineering to promote civil rights and equality, as well as bringing the over-mighty to account. They have been helped to do this because the money at the other end of the bar table has not generally been able to intimidate the plaintiffs with adverse orders for costs. They made better use of exemplary or punitive damages to offer up a real corrective to nasty corporations or government, very often a much more real corrective than may have been offered by a regulator. And they have maintained, and will maintain, their rights to have their claims against the great and powerful dealt with by a jury. If you tell an American trial lawyer that their right to a jury trial might be curtailed, the most polite response you will get is to ask whether you come from Mars. And you will have noticed that out of the four reasons why the Americans are better placed here, three of them are essentially procedural.

Inequality

We have seen from the common law that the Chancellors were originally members of the church who saw themselves as champions of the poor, even if they were anything but poor themselves. The office of Chancery used to have a sign:

> It is the refuge of the poor and afflicted, it is the altar and sanctuary for such as against the might of rich men, and the countenance of great men, cannot maintain the goodness of their cause.

All that changed and only the wealthy could afford to go to Chancery or anywhere else in the law.

The common law is as well served now by lawyers acting *pro bono*, or for legal aid, as it ever has been. The major threat now is probably ill-informed zealots in cardigans on rostered days on who want to do the impossible and legislate for benevolence and beneficence and make *pro bono* compulsory.

But judges are not doing enough to control the length of trials. It is not much good saying that you have a right to go to court if the court allows a more powerful party on the other side to drag it out until they break you emotionally or financially. This, too, is part of the argument for having such cases heard by a jury. Big government or a big corporation or a big union will be a lot slower to play the bully before a jury (assuming that the judge would allow it in any event). Among other things, the verdict could reflect the attitude of the jury to this conduct.

That is why, outside of the US, the great and powerful do their best to avoid a jury. Nothing would suit the barons of the press better than to have at least the assessment of damages in libel actions taken out of the hands of a jury. This could be the biggest win for the barons since *Magna Carta*. And that is exactly what the press barons got in Australia when six little state governments – as it happens, all purportedly representing the workers – went cap in hand to the barons and sold their subjects down the river.

Jurists sometimes ask if we should have a tort of insult or outrage (as Roman law did). One answer, the simplest and most sensible answer, may be found in our history. In commenting upon compensation for injury payable during Anglo Saxon times, Sir Frederick Pollock noticed that under a law of Elfward (in the 10th century) 'contumelious outrage' was visited 'with heavier fines than any but the gravest wounds'. Pollock then commented:

> In the modern common law compensation for insult, as distinct from actual bodily hurt, is arrived at only in a somewhat indirect fashion, by giving juries a free hand in the measure of damages.

Sometimes the answer is to create different kinds of tribunals to deal with disputes of lesser value in money. (There is no other criterion.) That this reverses the policy of Henry II to centralise the justice system in the Royal Courts is not of itself determinative, but we have to acknowledge that we are creating a system where there is one law for the rich and another for the poor. In doing so, we are acknowledging that we have failed most of those for whom the laws were created. We are also creating other classes of 'judges', and the notion of second-rate or cut-rate 'judges' is very, very dangerous indeed.

Education

We have seen that the legal profession and the bench came into being over many hundreds of years when the 'apprentices' were trained on the job, and became the barristers at the Inns of Court. For centuries room was reserved for the students in the courts and Mansfield used to address them directly. It is only recently – in the past few hundred years – that universities have got involved in legal education. The profession should still hold the say about who can accept fees for appearing as counsel in court or otherwise act as a lawyer.

Thanks largely to American influence, the law schools have taught law by reference to the decided cases. Whether they should give more training for the bar is a matter for discussion. But what we cannot duck is that students are being released into the profession who have not been taught grammar, logic, or legal or constitutional history. This appalling result is the fault of the profession – and it occurs in one way or another across the common law world. It is fatal to the continued existence of the profession as it has been handed down to us.

We are also short-selling the students. They are coming out and getting their training looking to go, for the most part, into some dreary exercise in wealth-dissipation like a subsidised merchant bank or an international accounting firm, when they could be groomed to partake in a profession which actually has done some good for people and has provided a decent way of life to its members. We are creating degrees of money-hungry, lift-dwelling, power-suited, playmakers rather than good professional lawyers, and this is to the detriment of both the profession and the rest of the community.

If we do not teach our students the facts of life of the law, what are they to think about how the law, this bright new toy of theirs, got here? That the stork brought it? You can gauge the decline in legal education and scholarship easily enough. In the wild west of America – Nebraska, no less – in the 19th century, Roscoe Pound gave courses in Roman Law, History of English Law, and Analytical and Comparative Jurisprudence. His two most read works now are *The Spirit of the*

Common Law and *Introduction to the Philosophy of Law*. Neither has any footnote.

Rights

The singular gift to us of the common law is the one workable way of defending basic human rights that the world has known. Sadly, the United States, which carried the banner on human rights, has not lived up to its past.

At the beginning of Chapter VIII, we saw that Sebastian Haffner, who was a law student in Germany when Hitler was rising to power, said that the Germans 'at the moment of truth … collectively and limply collapsed … and suffered a nervous breakdown'. It is very, very hard not to say precisely that of the American reaction to the successful bombing of the Twin Towers.

Guantanamo Bay is a moral black hole. It has also been worse than useless as a 'weapon of war'. Just as badly, the Americans have resorted to torture. This was last practised legally in England during the civil and religious strife during the time of the Stuarts. Before that, hundreds of years before, Fortescue said:

> And how inhuman must that law be, which does its utmost to condemn the innocent and convict the judge of cruelty. A practice so inhuman deserves not indeed to be called a law, but the high road to hell … The execution of the sentence of the law upon criminals is a task fit only for little villains to perform, picked out from amongst the refuse of mankind …

It was the memory of the Star Chamber that caused Maitland to reflect that English law had escaped 'the everlasting bonfire'. The contempt for the Inquisition and torture was and is deeply felt within the text of the common law. Its outlawry was a great victory of our law – yes, our law – for humanity. It is revolting that this victory should be put in peril by those who have never practised the law or fought a real war, but whose minds have been dimmed by a slogan that has the strength and value of sugar candy. To consent to apply torture is as basal a repudiation of our heritage as you could find.

Sir William Holdsworth said this about torture:

> Once torture has become acclimatized in a legal system, it spreads like an infectious disease. It saves the labour of investigation. It hardens and brutalizes those who have become accustomed to use it.

In a footnote he added a comment from Sir Leslie Stephen on the practice of police in India: 'It is far pleasanter to sit comfortably in the shade rubbing red pepper into a poor devil's eyes than to go about in the sun hunting up evidence'. Even in ancient Rome, where torture was applied routinely, the law was clear that evidence obtained by torture was to be received with caution.

Above all, torture is wrong because it is immoral. It is immoral because it is contrary to the teaching of the Sermon on the Mount. If that writ does not reach you, it is wrong because it is contrary to the teaching of Kant. It involves being cruel to others by treating them as means and not as ends in themselves. The claim that the end justifies the means is the fallback of people like Napoleon, Hitler and Stalin. The fact that we as lawyers have to apply the law in practice and not our moral judgment does not preclude our condemning conduct because it is immoral. Those who condone torture are 'the refuse of mankind'.

The survival of capital punishment is just as bad, but that is the Puritan and frontier mentality at work; torture is the result of a failure of moral nerve.

Juries

We have already commented on the decline of the jury. Except in the United States, this is perhaps the greatest failing and challenge of the common law.

The role of the jury in the administration of both the common law and the constitution is fundamental. Courts spend most of their time deciding whether people have been honest, careless, reasonable, or fair. As Holmes said:

> The question what a prudent man would do under given circumstances is then equivalent to the question what are the teachings of experience as to the dangerous character of this or that conduct under these or those circumstances; and as the teachings of experience are matters of fact, it is easy to see why the jury should be consulted with regard to them.

It may be that the teaching of experience goes beyond mere fact – it goes to customs, values, and standards, and it is much better to have these issues determined by a jury than by a sterilized product of the judicial cloister. And what you get is the unexaminable verdict of 'the country'.

Juries keep judges honest. They also keep them in touch and judges need to be kept in touch. Holdsworth said that the fact that the Chancellors sat without a jury was one of the reasons why they became so out of touch and the law of equity became so rigid. In truth, it is the jury that delivers the best and simplest kind of equity by applying the verdict of the people in the service of the law. Such a verdict is likely to be more in touch with humanity than the reasoned decree of a lawyer trained in equity and sheltered from the world behind the bench. Coke said that 'the jurors are chancellors'; they help to avoid what Aristotle called 'intelligence without passion' in the law.

You can tell those tribunals that do not have juries. Statutory tribunals or courts whose brushes with the common law are both incidental and occasional tend to develop a closed, clubby, in-house, professional look, removed from the people that they are there to serve.

The function of the jury is also to ensure that the people are involved in the administration of justice – in modern management parlance, they own the problem. Winston Churchill was no lawyer, but he knew the English and their Constitution as well as anybody:

Actual Decline and Likely Fall

> The jury system has come to stand for all we mean by English justice, because so long as a case has to be scrutinised by twelve honest men, defendant and plaintiff alike have a safeguard from arbitrary perversion of the law. It is this which distinguishes the law of English courts from Continental legal systems based on Roman law. Thus amidst the great process of centralisation the old principle was preserved and endures to this day, that law flows from the people, it is not given by the King.

Outside of America the legal profession has been to blame for surrendering the right to trial by jury in nearly all civil cases. The damage to the fabric and spirit of the law is already apparent. And now some people, who really should know better, are suggesting that it might be dispensed with in criminal cases. We would not suffer being deprived of the right to determine the fate of governments; we should not suffer being deprived of the right to determine the fate of law suits.

We have recent incontestable evidence of the supreme role of the jury in the administration of our justice. In three different countries in the common law world, juries have refused to follow the paranoia of their governments, and in cases of allegations of crimes said to involve terrorism against people who were entitled to feel that they were a part of a persecuted minority, juries have given mixed verdicts that were both reasonable and fair; and which were manifestly independent of any organ of government.

But, then, none of this is new. Lawyers rarely change, at least for the better. Just over a hundred years ago a calm summer evening session of the American Bar Association was rudely disturbed. An upstart lawyer from a hick prairie law school gave a paper *'The Causes of Popular Dissatisfaction with the Administration of Justice'*. And he really meant it! He electrified and then repelled that august body. His subjects included – 'A Multiplicity of Courts is a Characteristic of Archaic Law', 'Our Procedure is Behind the Times', 'Our Judicial Power is Wasted', 'The Worst Feature of Procedure is the Lavish Granting of New Trials', 'Our Legislation is Crude', 'Putting Courts into Politics has almost Destroyed the Traditional Respect for the Bench'. Well, the members of the ABA recovered their composure, and things went on as before. But something did follow the address. Dean Wigmore poached the speaker, Roscoe Pound, for North-Western, and later Dean Thayer poached him for Harvard. In those days gun legal scholars were as much sought after as gun footballers.

We might take our leave of juries, and the old medieval law, and indeed from this history, with a final reflection. The whole campaign of Henry V in France generated litigation in England. One suitor sought to attract jurisdiction in England by alleging that Harfleur was in Kent. At the battle of Agincourt, the French took heavy casualties. There was then litigation about ransoms. Robert Whittington, a mercer, sued a Frenchman, Stephen Turnebonis, for £296 as the ransom payable for a French prisoner taken at Agincourt, Hugh Coniers. The action was in a local court at London. The defendant appeared and said that the plaintiff had not been able to deliver. The plaintiff then asked that the matter be 'inquired of by the country' – that is, he sought a trial by jury. The defendant, who was not of that country, then asked that one half of the jurors should be aliens, and this was granted. If you look at the return of the names by the Serjeant, you will see that the 'aliens' have a decidedly un-Anglo Saxon lot of names compared to the 'denizens'.

As it happens, the Englishman recovered a judgment. But the defendant, the loser, should have been entitled to think he had got a fair run for his money. What more can you ask of any mode of trial? Is it possible that they may have done some things better back then in 1421? After all, for Frenchmen other than Monsieur Turnebonis, Agincourt was a sore point.

Chronology

(Many approximate)

2500	Code of Hammurabi (Babylon)
594	Laws of Solon (Athens)
451	Twelve Tables (Rome)
399	City of Athens *v* Socrates
33	Roman Empire *v* Jesus of Nazareth
415	Rome quits Britain
876–899	Alfred the Great (reign)
1066	Norman Conquest
1154–1189	Henry II (reign)
1180	Glanvill (*Laws of England*)
1215	Magna Carta
1210–1268	Life of Bracton
1377–1399	Richard II
1470	Fortescue, *In Praise of Laws*
1509–1547	Henry VIII
1603–1688	Four Stuarts (James I to James II)
1606–1616	Coke on bench
1628	Petition of Right
1688	Declaration of Rights
1689	Act for Declaration of Rights
1756–1788	Mansfield on bench
1765	Blackstone, *Commentaries*
1799–1827	Eldon on bench
1837–1901	Victoria
1882–1932	Holmes, judicial career
1944–1982	Denning, judicial career
2008	*DC v Heller*

Notes

I

fulfilled all justice: *Paradise Lost*, 5.246–7.
Cyclops: *The Odyssey*, 9, 125–29 (trans Fagles).
ancient customs: *Histories*, 2.41, 47, 68, 80.
Caste: **Maine**, *20*.
equity in Aristotle: *Nichomachean Ethics*, 1137a, 1143a, 1198b.
status to contract: **Maine**, 35 and 55.
lawyers of movement and resistance: **Maine**, 35, 55.

II

Inferno: *Canto*, 17. 21.
sanctity of king: **Holdsworth**, 2, 23.
root of title: **Holdsworth**, 2, 31.
involuntary loss: **Holdsworth**, 2, 79.
cattle theft: **Holmes**, 165.
form of oath: **Holdsworth**, 2, 107.

III

rule of writs: **Maitland**, 2, 563.
Churchman: **Holdsworth**, 2, 129–30.
Mr. Lynch: **Maitland**, *2*, 579–80.
exceptional vigour: **Maitland**, 2, 558–59.
plea of rape: **Glanvill**, 5, 175.
town meeting of judges: **Thayer**, 8.
stars before fight over: **Maitland**, 2, 634.
Milsom: **Maitland**, 1, Intro, ixvi–iii.
criterion of truth: **Blackstone**, 3, 348.
behaviour of judges: **Maitland**, 2, 620–71.
Holmes on law and logic: **Holmes**, 1 & 36.
everlasting bonfire: **Maitland**, 2, 658.

Notes

IV

royal favour: **Glanvill**, 28.
Magna Carta: **Holt**, 113.
commentary on Charter: **Stubbs**, 391.
King below law: **Maitland**, 1, 123.
due process: **Holdsworth**, 1, 62.
romanesque in form: **Maitland**, 1, 206–09.
King below law: **Bracton**, 1, 38.

V

Allen on Roman equity: **Allen**, 371–72.
too legal: **Allen**, 379.
do right: **Holdsworth**, 2, 337–39.
abuse of patron: **Story**, pars 48 & 50.
equity on bond: **Allen**, 385.
St. Germain: **Allen**, 391.
fees for length: **Baker**, 95–7.
ingenious pleading: **Allen**, 381.
jury and fiduciaries: *Equity*, 7.

VI

attorned: **Maitland**, 1, 211–13.
civic fathers: again, 216.
tough law: **Holdsworth** 2, 507, n.6.
Fortescue: **Fortescue**, Ch.3.
duty of serjeants: **Holdsworth**, 2, 486.
intellectual men: **Plucknett**, 220.
oratorical contest: **again, 222.**
formalism: **Winfield**, 156.
debating society: again.
examples from Year Books: **Holdsworth**, 2, 546–52.
Sam Weller: **Winfield**, 189n.
heroes of Year Books: **Plucknett**, 270.
Jews of Aden: **Winfield**, 146.
farrago of authorities: **Winfield**, 154.
dined at LC's: **Lemmings** 146–47.
seven Bishops: again, 145–52.
market forces: again, 259.

VII

bad form in crime: **Milsom**, 403.
transgression: **Maitland**, 2, 512.
capital rape: **Bracton**, 147–48b.
Stephen on crime: **Fifoot**, 123–24.
fix rights by agreement: **Maitland**, 2, 233.
private agreements: **Glanvill**, 132.
Aristotle: *Rhetoric*, 1375b, 23.

VIII

liberty of the subject: **Holdsworth**, 9, 118.
Dicey on de Tocqueville: **Dicey**, 108–09.
Judge-made constitution: **Dicey**, 116, 118.
Locke's theories: **Dunning**, 189.
practical political sagacity: **Dunning**, 192.
Churchill on Cromwell: *History of English Speaking People*, Vol. 2, 292.
no man who knows aught: **Milton's Prose**, (Scott Library), 66.
the tenure of kings: **again**, 68.

IX

Handsome for James 1: **Holdsworth**, 5, 434.
Stephen on Coke: **Holdsworth**, 5, 423.
loss of dignity: **Plunkett**, 49.
Sunday morning conference: **Spirit**, 74.
critics of Coke: **Holdsworth**, 5, 430.
alliance with Parliament: **Holdsworth**, 5, 444–5.
Trevelyan: *England under The Stuarts*, Folio, 1996, 105–06.
incarnate national dogmatism: cited in **Fifoot**, 229.
Murray as advocate: Fifoot, *Lord Mansfield*, 33.
adherence to status quo: **Melikan**, 210.
men of property: **Melikan**, 356.
Eldon's judgments: **Holdsworth**, 13, 624.
Jones on Holmes: *Dictionary*, 254.
German mind: **Holmes**, 206–7.
Danseuses and skirt dancing: **Holmes–Pollock Letters**, Harvard, 1942, Vol 2, 261.
Maitland on Maine: **Fifoot**, 54, 87 & 117.
almost feminine charm: **Goodhart**, 62.
Skill not won by chance: **Cardozo**, 172.
immunity of accused: **Spirit**, 105.
verbally beheaded: **Heuston**, 13.
Holdsworth on Dickens: **Holdsworth**, *Charles Dickens as a Legal Historian*, 112.

X

Duty to keep contract at common law: Holmes, *Collected Legal Papers*, New York, 1920, 127 (*The Path of the Law*).
Maxim of Kant: *The Moral Law*, Routledge, 1991, 97.
Analytical jurists: Pound, *Law and Morals*, OUP, 1924, 39.

XI

Wigmore's sporting theory: cited in **Pound**, 127.
Puritan jealousy of judge: **Pound**, Lecture II.
Standing on your own feet: **Pound**, 20.
Pound before Nebraska jury: **Sagre**, 94.
Legislation not keeping pace: **Maine**, 305.
Legal standard capable of being known: **Holmes**, 111.

Notes

Working knowledge and small change: cited in **Cardozo**, 97–98.
Raleigh v Coke: (1603) *State Trials* (1730) Vol 1, 205, 212.
Freed from contact with plain man: Maitland, *Essays*, 116.
Justice is never so safe: **Fortescue**, 212.
Compensation for insult: **Maitland** (chapter by Pollock), 1, 53.
Inhuman law: **Fortescue**, 73–74.
Everlasting bonfire; **Maitland**, 2, 658.
Torture infectious: **Holdsworth**, 5, 194–195.
What a prudent man would do: **Holmes**, 150.
Intelligence without passion: **Pound**, *Introduction*, 66, 68.
Churchill on juries: Churchill, above, Vol 1, 219.
Causes of popular dissatisfaction, see **Sagre**, 147ff.
Agincourt litigation: Fifoot, *History and Sources*, 314–315.

References

(Abbreviated titles referred to in the notes are in bold)

Allen, C.K.: *Law in the Making* (6th Ed), Oxford, 1958.
Ames, J. B.: *Lectures on Legal History,* Cambridge, 1913.
Baker, J.H.: *Introduction to English Legal History*, 2nd Ed, London, 1979.
Bowen, C.D.: *The Lion and the Throne*, Boston, 1956.
Blackstone, W.: *Commentaries on the Laws of England*, Oxfrod, 1765 (4 Vols).
Bracton, *On the Laws and Customs of England*, Ed Woodbine, Trans Thorne, Harvard, 1977 (4 Vols).
Buckland, W. W.: *Text-book of Roman Law,* 3rd Ed. Cambridge, 1963.
Denning, Lord: *The Family Story*, London, 1981.
Dicey, A.V.: *The Law of the Constitution 1915*, 8th Ed., Macmillan.
Dunning, W. R. : *Political Theory, Luther to Montesquieu,* Macmillan, 1923.
Feaver, G.: *From Status to Contract*, Longmans, 1969.
Fifoot, C.H.S.: *History and Sources of Common Law*, London, 1949.
Fifoot, C.H.S.: *Judge and Jurist in the Reign of Queen Victoria*, London, 1959.
Fifoot, C.H.S.: *Frederick William Maitland*, Harvard, 1971.
Fifoot, C.H.S.: *Lord Mansfield,* Oxford, 1936.
Fortescue, J.: *Laws of England*, Robert Clark & Co., 1874 (Legal Classics Library).
Glanvill,R.: *Laws and Customs of England*, Nelson 1965 (LCL).
Goodhart, A.L.: *Five Jewish Lawyers of the Common Law*, Oxford, 1949.
Hale, M.: *History of the Common Law*, London, 1713 (LCL).
Hart, H.L.A.: *Law, Liberty and Morality*, London, 1963.
Heuston, R.F.V.: *Lord Denning, The Man and his Times*, in *Lord Denning: The Judge and the Law*, Ed, Jowell & McAuslan, London, 1994.
Holdsworth, W.: *A History of English Law* 2nd Ed., London, 1936 (16 Vols).
Holdsworth, W.: *Charles Dickens as a Legal Historian*, Yale, 1928.
Holmes, O.W.: *The Common Law*, Boston, 1881 (LCL).
Holt, J.C.: *Magna Carta*, 2nd Ed., Cambridge, 1992.
Jones, G.: *History of the Law of Charity – 1532–1827*, CUP, 1969.
Macaulay, T.B.: *The History of England*, Folio, 1985 (2 Vols).
Maine, H.: *Ancient Law*, London 1861 (LCL).
Maitland, F.W.: *The Constitutional History of England*, Cambridge, 1963.
Maitland, F.W.: *Forms of Action at Common Law* (Sep Ed) 1936
Maitland, F.W.: *Equity,* 2nd Ed Rev, Cambridge, 1936
Melikan, R.A.: *John Scott, Lord Eldon*, Cambridge, 1999.

References

Milsom, S.F.C.: *Historical Foundations of the Common Law* (2nd Ed) London, 1981.
Oldham, J: *The Mansfield Manuscripts*, Uni, North Car., 1992 (2 Vols).
Novick, S.M.: *Honourable Justice*, Boston, 1989.
Pollock, F. and **Maitland**, F.W.: *The History of English Law Before the Time of Edward I*, Revised Ed, Cambridge, 1898 (2 Vols).
Pound, Roscoe: *The Spirit of the Common Law*, Boston, 1921 (LCL).
Pound, Roscoe: *Introduction to the Philosophy of Law*, Yale, 1954
Sagre, J : *Life of Roscoe Pound*, Iowa State University, 1948
Simpson, A.W.B.: *Biographical Dictionary of the Common Law*, London, 1984; *History of the Common Law of Contract*, Clarendon, 1975.
Stephenson & Marcham: *Sources of English Constitutional History*, New York, 1937.
Stubbs, W.: *Select Charters*, 9th Ed. (Davis), Oxford, 1913.
Thayer, J.B.: *Preliminary Treatise on the Law of Evidence at Common Law*, Boston, 1898.
Thomson, R.: *Magna Carta*: London, 1829 (LCL).
White, G.E.: *Justice Oliver Wendell Holmes*, Oxford, 1993
Windeyer, V.: *Lectures on Legal History* (2nd Ed) Law Book Co., 1957.
Year Books, 1 Edward I to 27 Henry VIII, 1679 Edition, 11 Volumes.

List of Cases

Abrams v. United States (1919) 250 US 616
Calthorpe's Case (1574) Dyer 334
Coggs v. Bernard (1703) 92 ER 107
Cole v Whitfield (1988) 165 CLR 360
District of Columbia v Heller (2008) 554 US
Doige's Case (1442) YB 20 Henry VI, f 34, pl. 4
Donoghue v Stevenson [1932] AC 562
Farrier's Case YB (1372) 46 Edw III, f 19 pl. 19
Fowler v Lanning [1959] 1 QB 426
Innkeeper's Case (1369) YB Easter 42 Ed 3, f 11, pl. 13
Marshal's Case (1441) 19 Henry VI 6, f 49, pl. 5
Macpherson v Buick Manufacturing (1916) 217 NY 582
Miller's Case (1367) YB Mich 41 Ed 3 f 24, pl. 17
Parker v R (1963) 111 CLR 610
Proudman v Dayman (1941) 67 CLR 536
Shaw v DPP [1962] AC 223
Surgeon's Case (1375) YB Hil 48 Ed 3, f 6, pl. 11
Waldon v Marshall (1370) YB Mich 43 Ed 3, f 33, pl. 38

Index

ABA 20
abuse of right 33
Act of Settlement 71
action on the case 61
Adam 1
Aethelbert 14
affidavits 38
Agincourt 128
Allen 33
Ames x
Anglo-Saxon 11–16, 27, 41
assumpsit 62
Athens 7, 10

Babylon 4
Bacon 35–6
Becket 79
Bill of Rights 2, 54, 71, 106
Blackstone 23, 71
Bonhoeffer x
Bracton 24, 31, 34
Burke, E 81

Caesar, Sir J 36
Cambridge 43
Canaries 89
carriers 63
Cardozo x, 89–91
Catherine of Aragon 31
chancery 20, 33ff, 53, 61
Charles I 8, 68
charters of land 13
chicane 33
Churchill 74, 128
Cibber 81
Coke 36, 52, 59, 77–81, 115, 117
Common pleas 53, 56, 77
confidence 36

Constitution 68–76
contract 60–66, 99 ff
Corpus Juris 3
Countess of Albermarle 48
covenant 61
crime 56–60, 96 ff
Cromwell 74

Dante 12
de Tocqueville 72
debt 60
Declaration of Independence 71, 103
delay 116ff
Denning, Lord 82, 85, 93–94
Dicey x, 72
Dickens 37, 84, 94–95
Dido 82
discovery 38
Disraeli 45
divine right 30
Doctors 44
Dunning 73, 76

Edward I 41–42
Egypt 3
Eldon, Lord 84–85
Elizabeth I 37, 69
Elfward 122
Ellesmere 35
English church 27
equity 5, 32–40
Essoin 15
Eton 51, 88
Eve 1
Evelyn 53

felonies 58
fiduciary 36ff

FitzWalter 26
Fortescue 42, 44
Franco 74
fraud (equity) 36
fusion 39, 114–116

Ghandi 45
Gibbon 52
Gladstone 54
Glanvill 19–20, 34, 57
Glorious Revolution 53, 54, 75
Golden Bull 28
Goodhart 91; Grand Jury 59
Gray, John 91
Gray's Inn 42, 47
Guantanamo Bay 73, 124

Habeas corpus 69, 73, 120
Haffner 74, 124
Hamlet 59, 116
Hammurabi 3
Hardwicke 35, 82
Hart, HLA 72
Harvard 48, 88, 91, 117,128
Hayle 59
Heath, C 103
Hegel 73
Henry II 19–24, 122
Henry VIII 31, 69
Herodotus 3
Hitler 74, 125
Holdsworth ix, x, 13, 18, 43, 59, 70, 72, 80, 85, 95, 125, 128
Holmes x, 14, 23, 67, 86–8, 111, 114
Homer 2
Hospitallers 42
Hudson, Sir E 73

Inner Temple 42, 77
innkeepers 63
Inns of Court 47–53, 123

James I 55, 81
James II 68
Jefferson 103
Jesus 7–8
jury 58, 125–127
Justinian 3, 6

Kant 86, 125
King John 25ff
King's Bench 53
King's Peace 13

Lemmings 54
Lincoln, A 45, 87
Lincoln's inn 42, 47
Locke 73
Louis Capet 8

Macaulay 74, 80, 89
Magic Flute 44
Magna Carta 2, 25–31, 60, 69, 70, 80, 116, 122
Maine x, 2, 5, 60, 67, 112
Maitland x, 14, 18, 22, 23, 29, 31, 39, 43, 45, 57, 60, 88–89, 111, 119, 124
Mandela 45
Mansfield 54, 63, 69, 81–83, 94, 123
Mao 74
Merits 108
Middle Temple 42
Milton 1
Milsom 23
Miranda 2
More 35
Murdoch 105

Napoleon 125
Nebraska 91, 108, 111
negligence 64–70
New Deal 91
Newman, Paul 52
Normans 18–24
Norris, Lord 69
Nottingham 35
Nuremberg 117

Oxford 43, 75, 93

Pares, R 53–4
personal actions 60
Petition of Right 71, 80
Pickwick Papers 50
Pilate, Pontius 8–9
Pirandello 99
Pleas of the Crown 56
Plucknett 45, 46, 51, 79
Pollock, F x, 17, 23, 87, 88–89, 122
Pound 91–92, 108, 111, 123, and 127–8
Pope, the 30
Praetor 33
Privilegio 28
pro bono 121

Quintilian 38

Index

Raleigh 78
Raphael 1
restitution 63
Richard I 19
Richelieu 71
Rome 4–10
Roosevelt 91
Rousseau 73
Rumpole 108
Runnymede 26

Saint Germain 36
Saint Paul 44
sclerosis 112ff
Sermon on the Mount 59
Seven Bishops 53
Serjeants 44ff
Shakespeare 2, 47, 93
Shylock 35
Simonds, Lord 40, 94
Simpson, O J 117
Socrates 7, 117
Solon 3, 106
Somerset 82
Stalin 125
Star Chamber 73, 79, 111, 124
status to contract 6
Statute of Westminster 61
Stephen, Sir J 59, 77, 88
Story 35, 38
subpoena 34

Tacitus 11, 12
Tchaikovsky 89
Templars 42
Thayer x, 128
Trespass 56–60
Trevelyan 80
trust 104ff
Twelve Tablets 3, 106

unconscionable 105
United States 9
unjust enrichment 63
utter barristers 43

Victoria (Q) 39, 115

Wagner, R 89
Walpole 54
Westminster 44, 120 (System)
Wigmore x, 111, 128
Wilkes 82
Winfield 47–8
witness statements 119ff
Wittgenstein 89
Wolsey 35
writs 17–24

year books ix, 46–50

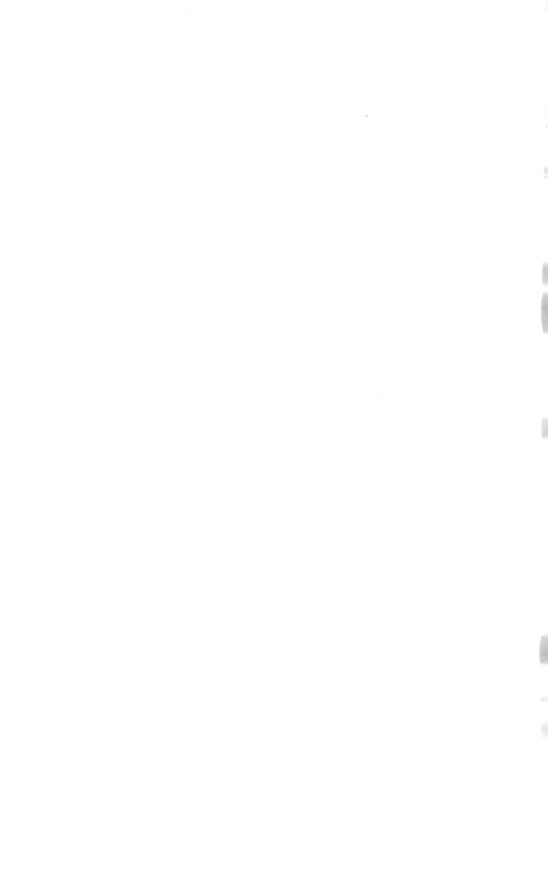